Confessing
the One Faith

Confessing the One Faith

An Ecumenical Explication of the Apostolic Faith

as it is confessed in the Nicene-Constantinopolitan Creed (381)

Faith and Order Paper No. 153
WCC Publications, Geneva

ISBN 2-8254-1036-5

© 1991 WCC Publications, World Council of Churches,
P.O. Box 2100
1211 Geneva 2, Switzerland

Fifth printing, corrected with a new preface, 1999

Website: http://www.wcc-coe.org

Cover design: Edwin Hassink

Printed in Switzerland

Table of Contents

Preface

Informed observers of church life have noted that, in recent decades, the churches have been affected by profound questioning about the content of their faith, and this has had important repercussions in ecumenical life. In view of the often discordant conclusions of the many forms of analysis to which Scripture is subjected, people are asking where to find those truths of faith which are the foundation of koinonia, and where to turn to find verification of the ecclesial doctrines which divide the churches. Even the most fundamental statements about the person of Christ and his work are being interpreted in different, sometimes contradictory ways. During one of the Padare sessions at the eighth assembly of the World Council of Churches in Harare in December 1998, participants said: "Tell us what we have to confess if we are genuinely to belong to the *una sancta*."

I. In Bangalore (1978), Lima (1982) and Stavanger (1985), the Commission on Faith and Order had already decided to press ahead with an in-depth study on the vast question of the common confession of the apostolic faith. The responses of several churches to the Lima document on *Baptism, Eucharist and Ministry* urged that this study be carried out as rapidly and as seriously as possible, for they realized that the churches cannot be truly united unless each recognizes in the life and practice of the others the fullness of the apostolic faith which it professes. For some churches, this applies even to the case of baptism in which the faith of the ages, understood in its most authentic sense, has to be proclaimed. The different expressions of confessional doctrine known since the Reformation as "confessions of faith" (Augsburg, La Rochelle, Westminster, Philadelphia, etc.) need to affirm that faith. The goal to be attained through this mutual *recognition* is the *common* confession (in the classical sense of the word) of the *common* apostolic faith, the source of the *koinonia* among the churches which is so much wanting today. This *common* confession could then form the basis for all the other measures necessary for the return to visible unity.

Obviously, each church must ask itself in all honesty and sincerity in how far, in its liturgical practice and its life of witness to the Gospel, but also more immediately in its preaching and catechesis, it is in total harmony with what the churches in *communion* have from the beginning confessed as the *true* faith. In how far is it faithful to the integrity of this faith? If it discovers itself to be unfaithful, in that it adheres only to "chosen pieces" of the given of faith or to "expurgated dogmas" (*sic*), it is in need of renewal.

This examination of conscience is more necessary than ever today, for a number of reasons. On the one hand, fundamentalist movements are springing up all over the place, many of them questioning official teachings which they consider too vague or too liberal, and on the other, new opinions are creating a certain perplexity, even anxiety in the churches. Is Jesus Christ the divine actor in a fairy tale, a preacher and instigator of an altruistic moral code, a likeable man deified after the event by his disciples – or is he the One celebrated in the liturgies of the Nativity and of Easter? Is the Church simply a human association of "friends of Jesus" or does it have its origin in God's purpose of leading humanity to communion in his Trinitarian life? Is the hope of eternal life simply a grandiose dream?

II. 1. An examination of this sort aiming at recognition of the faith and its present state in the churches in search of visible unity, requires tools and instruments to guide it. For this purpose, the Commission on Faith and Order, after a consultation held in Rome in October 1983, chose to offer the churches an explication of – or extended commentary on – the ecumenical Creed of Nicea and Constantinople (381), received by the Council of Chalcedon (451) as bearing witness to the traditional faith.

The Commission was of course aware of the position of some churches which do not use credal statements, either for fear it may lead to formalism at the expense of the personal commitment of individual Christians to their faith, or because they do not want to put pressure on consciences. But it also knew that the doctrine of these churches corresponds in fact to what is expressed in the articles of the Creed. As the primary aim was not to impose the use of the latter but only to present its doctrine, this choice did not violate the traditions of those churches.

Moreover, the Commission had been at pains to elicit studies in which Christian communities of different languages and cultures and various traditions expressed the baptismal faith in their own words. The essential thing was the content. It did not, however, abandon the hope that, in certain circumstances, all the churches might unite in reciting together the Nicene-Constantinopolitan Creed – which would be a magnificent sign of koinonia in the faith.

2. Why was this Creed chosen? At a time when erroneous positions on Christ and the Holy Spirit were already tearing the Church apart, the Ecumenical Councils set forth the faith of the apostolic community which it is the Church's mission to safeguard, defend and transmit. The essential truths of this faith were summarized and articulated in creeds or confessions of faith, most often in the liturgical context of baptism.

The credal statement known as the Nicene-Constantinopolitan Creed is a typically Eastern creed, the core of which dates back to the Council of Nicea (325), while its third article is linked with the Council of Constantinople (381). Because it is used in the liturgies of both East and West it is undoubtedly the best witness to the unity of the churches in the apostolic faith, as Faith and Order affirmed at Lausanne (1927). It reminds all Christians and all communities of their faith, and links it with the faith of all ages and all places. The churches of the Reformation have included it in their credal books as a reference text that objectively expresses the faith, making no concessions to religious sentimentality, and drawing directly on Scripture.

3. Faith and Order presents the text of this Creed and offers an explication of its content. The latter is the fruit of long and painstaking work entrusted to a small team called the Steering Group. But the group did not work all by itself, indeed it was concerned to involve as many theologians of all confessions and denominations as possible, through international consultations and meetings. Besides this, a first draft of the study document, published in 1987 (Faith and Order Paper no. 140), brought an impressive number of reactions, comments and suggestions from members of the Commission, theologians, theological faculties, ecumenical institutes, ecumenical conferences, national Faith and Order commissions, and National Councils of Churches. This material was carefully examined and further developed by the Steering Group over a period of more than three years. In 1990 at Dunblane (Scotland), the Standing Commission approved the new version of the document, entirely revised and corrected on this basis. It authorized its publication

and the study document was duly sent to the churches for further study and consideration.

4. This is not a consensus, nor even a convergence text, but an instrument offered to the churches to assist them as they reflect on and seek to recognize the apostolic faith. This is why we were careful to include in each section an "explication for today", intended to present the traditional doctrine in language appropriate for our times.

III. 1. To assist the churches in this reflection on the common faith, the meeting of the Standing Commission (known at that time as the Board) in Bangkok in 1996 approved the publication of a small study guide for use in group discussions or for more personal study. This small, 30-page booklet is written in very simple language, avoiding too many technical terms and including frequent references to the major biblical texts. It is intended to be accessible to all circles in the churches and seeks to link the Creed to questions of faith and practice, without addressing these directly, following the literary genre of the catechism. Its aim is above all pastoral.

This document should not be taken as a substitute for the study "Confessing the One Faith", however. It can serve as a helpful introduction to reading the latter and understanding its structure, but it cannot replace it. Especially in the very complex situation described above, the churches, and above all the men and women who carry particular responsibility for the teaching and safeguarding of the faith, cannot content themselves with this shorter instrument. It was not written to provide all the light they need for examining the confession of the apostolic faith.

2. After a hiatus of three years while we awaited the responses of the churches, the time has now come to relaunch the programme "Towards a Common Expression of the Apostolic Faith Today". For this it was felt that a second edition of our working tool, the study "Confessing the One Faith", should be prepared. Several reactions from participants in the Padare sessions at Harare – which unfortunately cannot be included in the official record of the eighth assembly because of the way these meetings were designed – expressed deep concern about the state of the faith in the churches. By its very vocation, Faith and Order is directly challenged here. With its study on hermeneutics, *A Treasure in Earthen Vessels* (1998), which deals directly with the question of interpreting Scripture and the sources for communities living in different contexts, it clarified the method that will guide our thinking. The paper on "The Nature and Purpose of the Church" (1998) emphasized the need to reach a common understanding of Christian identity

in a changing world (cf. no. 120). The ground has thus been laid for each church to set to work, taking to heart the questions being asked by its members, conscious of the growing malaise, and united with all the churches in their anxiety about "the future of the faith". Faith and Order knows that no-one can abdicate before a problem of this kind. It is a matter of our faithfulness to God himself. Will Christians one day be able to declare together before the world, in common confession and praise, their faith in who God is and what God has done?

IV. 1. *Confessing the One Faith* is structured in three *parts*, following the three articles of the Creed. Each part consists of sections focusing on the main themes of each article. Further sub-divisions correspond to specific phrases in the text of the Creed that need explanation.

2. Each *section* begins with introductory paragraphs indicating basic affirmations as well as main challenges to be faced with regard to the respective theme. In identifying these challenges attention is paid to three crucial factors:

- the language and philosophy of the age in which the creeds were formulated are no longer those of the present day;
- the influence of old and new religions is more and more affirmed and appreciated in many cultures;
- in modern societies, especially with the process of secularization, many of the basic affirmations of the Christian faith are questioned.

Subsection I for each article presents historical and biblical interpretations. It starts by citing the respective passages of the Nicene and the Apostles' Creeds. It continues with a few explanatory notes on the credal formulations and concludes with biblical aspects which are foundational for the respective themes.

Subsection II in each case concentrates on the "explication for today". It starts with the assertions of the Creed, trying to present an accurate interpretation of the words used in their historical context. But in doing so, an attempt is made to use vocabulary intelligible in the present time. Even if the historical sources are never quoted, they were always taken into consideration. Thus the explication follows the phrases of the Nicene Creed and relates the subject matter to challenges of today in order to interpret the respective aspect of the apostolic faith for our present time.

3. In some places *commentaries* are added. These contain either additional historical background information or theological details or continuing controversial themes. *Italics* indicate the themes of the para-

graphs, and sometimes also the focus of the interpretation. The paragraphs of the whole explication are *numbered* in order to facilitate their citation.

Finally there are the *appendices* which include a historical survey on the study, a glossary which may be useful for those who are not familiar with some of the technical terms and which may provide a historical, theological or ecumenical meaning for further use, and a list of consultations and meetings related to the whole process of this study (including a list of those who contributed to and participated in these meetings). The short selective bibliography is strictly related to the Apostolic Faith study programme, giving preference to WCC publications.

4. The translation of the Nicene Creed used in the first edition of *Confessing the One Faith*, taken from the International Consultation on English Texts (ICET), has been shown to be problematic, particularly in the phrase relating to the incarnation. This translation has since been altered by the current English Language Liturgical Consultation (ELLC) in order to be more faithful to the original Greek text of the Creed. The passage which, in the first edition, reads

> by the power of the Holy Spirit
> he became incarnate from the Virgin Mary

now reads

> was incarnate of the Holy Spirit and the Virgin Mary.

5. We are grateful to all who contributed to the development of this document, to the Faith and Order Commission and especially to the Apostolic Faith Steering Group members: without their deep commitment and untiring work this document could not have been brought to fruition.

Our deep gratitude is due to the directors of the Secretariat, Rev. Dr Günther Gassmann (1984-95) and Rev. Dr Alan Falconer (since 1995), to the responsible staff, Rev. Dr Hans-Georg Link (1982-86), V. Rev. Prof. Dr Gennadios Limouris (1986-93), and Dr Peter Bouteneff (since 1995). Special gratitude is due to Yemba Kekumba who moderated the preparation of the Study Guide *Towards Sharing the One Faith*, and to Mrs Renate Sbeghen for her exemplary assistance and administrative help. They have all worked in a spirit of fellowship and with profound ecumenical commitment to the goal of the unity of the Church.

JEAN-MARIE TILLARD OP
Moderator of the Apostolic Faith Steering Group

Introduction

A. THE GOAL OF VISIBLE UNITY

1. The primary function and purpose of the World Council of Churches is "to call the churches to the goal of visible unity in one faith and in one eucharistic fellowship" (Constitution of WCC, III,1). Three essential conditions and elements of visible unity have been identified:
— the common confession of the apostolic faith;
— the mutual recognition of baptism, eucharist and ministry;
— common structures for witness and service as well as for decision-making and teaching authoritatively.
The Lima text on *Baptism, Eucharist and Ministry*[1] and the responses of the churches to the text have already contributed towards the second essential element of visible unity. The present project of Faith and Order is intended to help the churches move towards the common confession of the apostolic faith.

B. TOWARDS THE COMMON EXPRESSION
OF THE APOSTOLIC FAITH TODAY: THE PROJECT

2. The first steps in developing the project were taken at the meeting of the Faith and Order Commission in *Bangalore* in 1978. The project was given further direction at the meetings in *Lima* in 1982 and in *Stavanger* in 1985.
3. The title of the project *Towards the Common Expression of the Apostolic Faith Today* refers in the first instance to the ecumenical

---

[1] *Baptism, Eucharist and Ministry*, Faith and Order Paper No. 111, WCC, Geneva, 1982.

commitment to move towards confessing together the one apostolic faith that is attested in the Holy Scriptures and summarized in the creeds of the early Church. This same faith should be *expressed* together today: it should be witnessed to, confessed, and celebrated in *common* (both corporately and together as churches of different traditions). The faith has to be confessed in different situations and in relation to the challenges of the world *today*.

4. The project on the apostolic faith aims at serving the endeavours of the churches to manifest their visible unity and also to fulfil their calling to confess their faith in common mission and service to the world. As the 1983 Vancouver assembly of the World Council of Churches stated, "... the churches would share a common understanding of the apostolic faith, and be able to confess this message together in ways understandable, reconciling and liberating to their contemporaries".[2] The aim of the project is not to formulate a new ecumenical creed.

5. In order to respond to their calling, churches which belong to different Christian traditions and live in diverse cultural, social, political and religious contexts, need to reappropriate their common basis in the apostolic faith so that they may confess their faith together. In so doing, they will give common witness to the saving purposes of the Triune God for all humanity and all creation. The apostolic faith must always be confessed anew and interpreted in the context of changing times and places: it must be in continuity with the original witness of the apostolic community and with the faithful explication of that witness throughout the ages.

6. The unity of the churches requires mutual trust. In the full communion which churches are looking for, each church must be able to recognize in the other the fullness of the apostolic faith. This does not mean a complete identity of interpretation of the apostolic faith. Nevertheless a degree of unanimity is required for the mutual recognition of the apostolic faith, while allowing for a measure of difference in the interpretation of that faith.

7. The term *apostolic faith* used in this study does not refer to a single fixed formula, nor to a specific moment in Christian history. Rather, it points to the dynamic reality of the Christian faith. The faith is grounded in the prophetic witness of the people of the Old Testament, and in the

---

[2] *Gathered for Life. Official Report. VI Assembly of World Council of Churches*, Vancouver, Canada (24 July-10 August 1983), ed. D. Gill, WCC/Wm. B. Eerdmans, Geneva/ Grand Rapids, 1983, p.45.

normative testimony, reflected in the New Testament, of the apostles and those who proclaimed together with them the gospel in the early days (apostolic age) and in the testimony of their community. The apostolic faith is expressed in confession, in preaching, in worship and in the sacraments of the Church as well as in the credal statements, decisions of councils and confessional texts and in the life of the Church. Theological reflection has always rendered a service to the confessing community by seeking to clarify the faith.

8. The central affirmations of the apostolic faith were set out in a particular way in the credal statements of the early Church. These ancient creeds continue to function within the context of the life of faith of many of the churches. In a special way this is true of the Ecumenical Creed of Nicea and Constantinople (381) in distinction from other creeds of regional authority. And, even in churches where the ancient credal statements are not regularly used, the faith to which they bear witness is confessed and lived.

9. The Apostolic Faith study is related to the two other major Faith and Order programmes. It seeks to provide a wider basis and framework for the Lima document with its ecclesiological focus on "Baptism, Eucharist and Ministry" and takes up insights from this text and from the responses of the churches to it. The ecclesiological focus of the study on "The Unity of the Church and the Renewal of Human Community" will be enriched by the broader Trinitarian perspective on God's salvific action in creation, redemption and fulfilment set out in the Apostolic Faith study. In its reference to present-day challenges the Apostolic Faith study will profit from the reflection of the Unity/ Renewal study on specific situations of human brokenness crying out for renewal.

C. THE METHOD OF THE STUDY PROJECT

I. Explication

10. The Faith and Order Commission, at Lima in 1982, decided to develop this study of the Apostolic Faith at three levels: *common recognition, explication and confession of the apostolic faith*. But later, at a consultation in Rome in October 1983, it was felt that the *explication* should be the starting point of the project and a special emphasis in the study because it is the presupposition for reaching the goal of a common recognition and confession of the apostolic faith in our time.

11. The explication seeks to indicate the relevance of basic convictions of the Christian faith in the face of some particular *challenges* of our time and world. It seeks to discover and formulate *basic* insights which can be understood and accepted by Christians from different traditions, but does not pretend to solve all theological differences. It integrates biblical, historical and contemporary perspectives and relates doctrinal affirmations to a number of today's problems.

12. The Faith and Order Commission decided, in order to identify the fundamentals of the apostolic faith which should be explicated, to use the *Nicene-Constantinopolitan Creed of 381*[3] as the theological and methodological tool. This Creed:

— has been more universally received than any other symbol of the faith, as a normative expression of the essential content of the apostolic faith;
— is part of the historical heritage of contemporary Christianity;
— has been in liturgical use through the centuries to express the one faith of the Church.

The Nicene Creed thus serves to indicate whether the faith as set forth in modern situations is the same faith as the one the Church confessed through the centuries.

13. The so-called "non-credal" churches have been particularly sensitive to the dangers of credal formulas. These formulas easily degenerate into formalism, at the expense of the nature of faith as personal confession and commitment. They may also be misused when their acceptance is enforced upon persons, thus violating their consciences. The choice made by Faith and Order to take the Nicene Creed as the basis of this study does not mean to demand the acceptance and use of the Nicene Creed, or indeed of any other credal formula, by the "non-credal" churches in their regular worship. Nevertheless, in assuming that they share the apostolic faith expressed in the Nicene Creed, it is hoped that, at least on special occasions, representatives of these churches can join in the profession of the Nicene Creed as a witness to their communion in the faith of the *one, holy, catholic and apostolic Church.*

14. The Nicene Creed is only one among many creeds which, since New Testament times, have been recognized as necessary to the Church for the formulation and recognition of its faith. Creeds summarize and

---

[3] In the following the "Nicene-Constantinopolitan Creed (381)" will be referred to as the "Nicene Creed".

focus on the essential contents of the apostolic faith. Many of them were developed in close connection with baptism.

15. In baptism a profession of faith is given according to the Trinitarian content of the faith of the community *(regula fidei)* which is at the same time recognized by the community. The profession of faith occurs also in those churches which do not formally use the words of the Nicene Creed when baptismal confession uses other formulas authorized by the Church. Here, likewise, baptismal confession joins the faith of the baptized to the common faith of the Church through the ages. The same faith is also expressed in the eucharistic liturgy by the confession of creeds.

16. The Nicene Creed is a conciliar creed which, by its wide reception, became the ecumenical symbol of the unity of the Church in faith. This function of the Nicene Creed as an ecumenical symbol was recognized by Faith and Order as early as Lausanne, 1927. While the so-called Apostles' Creed, which originated from Rome, has been received and used only in the Christian West, the Nicene Creed unites all parts of the Christian Church, East and West.

17. The affirmations of the Nicene Creed are rooted in the witness of the Holy Scriptures and must be tested against them and explicated in their light, within the context of the Tradition of the Church. Accordingly, the explication will seek to respond to the question as to what degree and in which form the fundamentals of the apostolic faith as witnessed to by the Holy Scriptures, proclaimed in the Tradition of the Church, and expressed in the Creed, can be commonly understood and expressed by churches of different confessional traditions, living in different cultural, social, economical, political and religious contexts.

II. Recognition

18. The process of recognition implies that each church is called to recognize:
— the apostolic faith in its own life and practice;
— the need for repentance *(metanoia)* and renewal as a consequence of seeing where they are not faithful to the apostolic faith;
— other churches as churches where the apostolic faith is proclaimed and confessed.

19. Accordingly, *Confessing the One Faith* is not intended to represent a consensus or even convergence document which could as such provide a basis for the common recognition and confession of the apostolic faith as an essential element of visible unity among the chur-

ches. Rather, this study document should be seen as an instrument to help the churches to focus on and reflect together upon the apostolic faith. Such study and reflection should lead towards a fresh understanding of the apostolic faith and thus towards a common recognition and confession of this faith today.

20. Recognition, therefore, has in this study process a very specific meaning. Each church has first to become aware how much in its own life and commitment it is faithful to the apostolic faith and how far it is confessing it in its words and deeds. At the same time every church that is committed to visible unity needs to recognize the fidelity to the apostolic faith in the confessional statements, liturgical life and witness, proclamation and practice of other churches. Bilateral and multilateral dialogues provide a means for this mutual discernment which leads to acts of common recognition of the apostolic faith.

21. Although the historical context of the formulation of the Nicene Creed is different from our present context, nevertheless the Nicene Creed remains a most appropriate text to help every church to recognize, in the particular situation of its own time and circumstance, the unchanging faith of the Church.

III. Confession

22. Common confession of the apostolic faith is one of the three essential conditions of visible unity. Common explication and recognition of the apostolic faith opens the way and provides a basis for a common confession of this same faith. This confession will ultimately require the mutual recognition of baptism, eucharist and ministry and the common structures for decision-making and teaching authoritatively. In such confession the churches will joyfully praise together their one God, Father, Son and Holy Spirit, the only source of their life and hope. In such common confession they will also respond together to the challenges which they are confronted with in specific situations and in our present world as a whole.

23. Already representatives of the churches are able to recite their faith together when they meet in ecumenical services. They say the Nicene or Apostles' Creed together or confess their faith in another form. This is an expression of their existing unity given in Christ. Yet this unity is contradicted by the lack of visible communion; in many cases those who recite their faith together belong to churches which are still divided.

24. Acts of common confession are, therefore, a challenge and encouragement to the churches to deepen their faithfulness to the apos-

tolic faith and thereby to move closer to each other. This movement has to be accompanied by other efforts towards visible unity in the form of theological dialogue and common commitment to God's will for humanity.

25. To engage in acts of common confession on behalf of the churches, especially in opening a Council, is more than an individual act as already happens in ecumenical gatherings. It requires the confidence that all the churches, which the participants represent in confessing the Creed, express the same faith. The purpose of this common explication of the Nicene Creed is to increase mutual confidence so that all churches may be helped to recognize the apostolic faith in each other.

26. When the churches are able, as a result of this broader movement, to confess their faith together, this will constitute one essential and integral expression of the unity we seek. United in one eucharistic fellowship and held together by common bonds of fellowship, they will be able to speak with one voice in confronting the burning issues of humanity. Then they will confess their faith together as part of their common life and witness.

27. Such common confession in the context of shared life will be made before God. At the same time it will become the fundamental source for a credible — because united — witness in the world. And in the deepest sense it would become a sign pointing to God's will for all of humanity to be reconciled in Christ and to be drawn finally into God's kingdom when all will confess and praise God without end.

D. AN INSTRUMENT OF RECOGNITION: CONFESSING THE ONE FAITH

I. Provenance of the text

28. The *Confessing the One Faith* study document has been developed since 1981/82 by means of a series of international consultations, extensive discussion at the 1985 meeting of the Faith and Order Commission in Stavanger, Norway, as well as at the 1989 meeting of the Faith and Order Commission in Budapest, Hungary, and consideration in the Standing Commission on Faith and Order, and especially in its Steering Group for this study.[4]

---

[4] See Appendices I and IV.

29. The first stage of work led to the provisional study document *Confessing One Faith*, published in 1987 (Faith and Order Paper No. 140). This text received a considerable number of reactions from individuals, meetings and commissions in churches and ecumenical bodies as well as from theological faculties. These reactions and a series of further consultations and discussions in the Standing and Plenary Commissions marked the second stage of work which led to a thorough revision of the document by the Steering Group. With the authorization of the 1990 Standing Commission the revised document is now published under the slightly expanded title *Confessing the One Faith* in order to emphasize that what is under consideration is the one faith of the Church through the ages. In some of the translations of the earlier version this emphasis was already clear.

30. As in the BEM process and in the responses of the churches to BEM it was recognized that particular difficulties, e.g. language and translation of such a text, exist for some regions of the world. In order to broaden participation in the study of the apostolic faith and of *Confessing the One Faith*, the Standing Commission, at Dunblane in 1990, authorized the preparation of a (short) "Study Instrument" to be completed by 1992.

31. This common explication is a theological document, formulated in an affirmative and explanatory manner. It addresses all the churches and within them particularly those who carry special responsibility for teaching the faith of the Church. It aims at assisting them to move towards the common recognition and confession of the apostolic faith today.

II. Structure of the text

32. *Confessing the One Faith* is structured in three *parts*, following the three articles of the Creed. Each part consists of sections focusing on the main themes of each article. Further sub-divisions correspond to specific phrases in the text of the Creed that need explication.

33. Each *section* begins with introductory paragraphs which indicate basic affirmations as well as main challenges to be faced with regard to the respective theme. In identifying these challenges attention is paid to three crucial factors:

— the language and philosophy of the age in which the creeds were formulated are no longer those of the present day;
— the influence of old and new religions is more and more affirmed and appreciated in many cultures;

— in modern societies, especially with the process of secularization, many of the basic affirmations of the Christian faith are questioned.

Sub-section I presents historical and biblical interpretations. It starts by quoting the respective passages of the Nicene and the Apostles' Creeds. It continues with a few explanatory notes on the credal formulations and concludes with biblical aspects which are foundational for the respective themes.

Sub-section II concentrates on the "explication for today". It starts with the assertions of the Creed, trying to present an accurate interpretation of the words used in their historical context. But in doing so, an attempt is made to use vocabulary intelligible in the present time. Even if the historical sources are never quoted, they were always taken into consideration. Thus the explication follows the phrases of the Nicene Creed and relates the subject matter to challenges of today in order to interpret the respective aspect of the apostolic faith for our present time.

34. In some places *commentaries* are added. They contain either additional historical background information or theological details or continuing controversial themes. *Italics* indicate the themes of the paragraphs, and sometimes also the focus of the interpretation. The paragraphs of the whole explication are *numbered* in order to facilitate their quotation.

APPENDICES

In the last part are the appendices which include a historical survey on the study, a glossary which may be useful for those who are not familiar with some of the technical terms and which may provide a historical, theological or ecumenical meaning for further use, and a list of consultations and meetings related to the whole process of the study (including a list of those who contributed and participated in these meetings). The short selective bibliography is strictly related to the Apostolic Faith study programme, giving preference to WCC publications.

The Texts of the Creeds

The Nicene-Constantinopolitan Creed

Text of 381 A.D.[1]

Πιστεύομεν εἰς ἕνα Θεόν, Πατέρα, παντοκράτορα,
ποιητὴν οὐρανοῦ καὶ γῆς,
ὁρατῶν τε πάντων καί ἀοράτων.

Καὶ εἰς ἕνα Κύριον Ἰησοῦν, Χριστόν,
τὸν Υἱὸν τοῦ Θεοῦ, τὸν μονογενῆ,
τὸν ἐκ τοῦ Πατρὸς γεννηθέντα πρὸ πάντων τῶν αἰώνων.
φῶς ἐκ φωτός, Θεὸν ἀληθινὸν ἐκ Θεοῦ ἀληθινοῦ,
γεννηθέντα οὐ ποιηθέντα, ὁμοούσιον τῷ Πατρί,
δι’ οὗ τὰ πάντα ἐγένετο.
Τὸν δι’ ἡμᾶς τοὺς ἀνθρώπους καὶ διὰ τὴν ἡμετέραν σωτηρίαν
κατελθόντα ἐκ τῶν οὐρανῶν
καὶ σαρκωθέντα ἐκ Πνεύματος Ἁγίου καὶ Μαρίας τῆς Παρθένου
καὶ ἐνανθρωπήσαντα.
Σταυρωθέντα τε ὑπὲρ ἡμῶν ἐπὶ Ποντίου Πιλάτου
καὶ παθόντα καὶ ταφέντα.
Καὶ ἀναστάντα τῇ τρίτῃ ἡμέρᾳ κατὰ τὰς Γραφάς.

---

[1] Greek text in *Enchiridion Symbolorum. Definitionum et Declarationum de Rebus Fidei et Morum*, ed H. Denzinger, 37th ed. Freiburg, 1991, pp. 83-85, No. 150.

Καὶ ἀνελθόντα εἰς τοὺς οὐρανούς,
καὶ καθεζόμενον ἐκ δεξιῶν τοῦ Πατρός.
Καὶ πάλιν ἐρχόμενον μετὰ δόξης κρῖναι ζῶντας καὶ νεκρούς,
οὗ τῆς Βασιλείας οὐκ ἔσται τέλος.

Καὶ εἰς τὸ Πνεῦμα τὸ Ἅγιον, τὸ Κύριον, τὸ Ζωοποιόν,
τὸ ἐκ τοῦ Πατρὸς ἐκπορευόμενον,
τὸ σὺν Πατρὶ καὶ Υἱῷ συμπροσκυνούμενον καὶ συνδοξαζόμενον,
τὸ λαλῆσαν διὰ τῶν Προφητῶν.
Εἰς μίαν, ἁγίαν, καθολικὴν καὶ ἀποστολικὴν Ἐκκλησίαν.
Ὁμολογοῦμεν ἓν βάπτισμα εἰς ἄφεσιν ἁμαρτιῶν.
Προσδοκῶμεν ἀνάστασιν νεκρῶν,
καὶ ζωὴν τοῦ μέλλοντος αἰῶνος. Ἀμήν.

We believe in one God,[2]
    the Father, the Almighty,
    maker of heaven and earth,
    of all that is, seen and unseen.

We believe in one Lord, Jesus Christ,
    the only Son of God,
    eternally begotten of the Father,
    Light from Light,
    true God from true God,
    begotten, not made,
    of one Being with the Father;
    through him all things were made.

---

[2] English text in *Praying Together,* a revision of *Prayers We Have in Common* (ICET 1975), agreed liturgical texts prepared by the English Language Liturgical Consultation 1988, Norwich, Canterbury Press, 1988, p. 9. The text here has been slightly altered to conform with the Greek original.

For us humans and for our salvation
  he came down from heaven,
  was incarnate of the Holy Spirit and the Virgin Mary,
  and was made human.
  For our sake he was crucified under Pontius Pilate;
  he suffered death and was buried.
  On the third day he rose again
  in accordance with the scriptures;
  he ascended into heaven
  and is seated at the right hand of the Father.
  He will come again in glory to judge the living
  and the dead,
  and his kingdom will have no end.

We believe in the Holy Spirit, the Lord, the giver of life,
  who proceeds from the Father and the Son,
  is worshipped and glorified,
  who has spoken through the Prophets.

We believe in one holy catholic and apostolic Church.
  We acknowledge one baptism for the forgiveness of sins.
  We look for the resurrection of the dead,
    and the life of the world to come. Amen

The Apostles' Creed

Credo in Deum[3]
Patrem omnipotentem,
creatorem caeli et terrae,

---

[3] Latin text in *Enchiridion Symbolorum, op. cit.*, p. 36, No. 30.

et in Iesum Christum,
    Filium eius unicum, Dominum nostrum,
    qui conceptus est de Spiritu Sancto,
        natus ex Maria virgine,
    passus sub Pontio Pilato,
        crucifixus, mortuus et sepultus,
    descendit ad inferna,
    tertia die resurrexit a mortuis,
    ascendit ad caelos,
        sedet ad dexteram Dei Patris
        omnipotentis,
    inde venturus est
        iudicare vivos et mortuos.

Credo in Spiritum Sanctum.
    sanctam Ecclesiam catholicam,
    sanctorum communionem,
    remissionem peccatorum,
    carnis resurrectionem,
    et vitam aeternam. Amen

I believe in God,[4] the Father almighty,
    creator of heaven and earth

I believe in Jesus Christ, God's only Son, our Lord,
    who was conceived by the Holy Spirit,
    born of the Virgin Mary,
    suffered under Pontius Pilate,
    was crucified, died, and was buried;
    he descended to the dead.
    On the third day he rose again;
    he ascended into heaven,
    he is seated at the right hand of the Father,
    and he will come again to judge the living and the dead.

---

[4] English text in *Praying Together, op. cit.*, p. 16.

I believe in the Holy Spirit,
    the holy catholic Church,
    the communion of saints,
    the forgiveness of sins,
    the resurrection of the body,
    and the life everlasting.

Explication : to explain and interpret in great detail.

WE BELIEVE

1. The Nicene Creed begins with the confident affirmation "We believe in" *(pisteuomen eis)* referring to Father, Son and Holy Spirit and to the one, holy, catholic and apostolic Church.

2. The first person plural "we believe" of the Nicene Creed differs from the "I believe" of the Apostles' Creed, of baptismal and some eucharistic liturgies. In baptism individuals, or those who speak on their behalf, respond to God's prevenient act of grace in a personal testimony of faith. The believer, through water and in the power of the Holy Spirit, is baptized into Christ's death and resurrection and brought into the communion of the Church. The individual's confession of faith, however, is made in communion with the confession of faith of the whole Church. Some local churches respond: "This is the faith of the Church, this is our faith."

3. The Nicene Creed as a confession of faith belongs to the one, holy, catholic and apostolic Church. In the Nicene Creed the individual joins with all the baptized gathered together in each and every place, now and throughout the ages, in the Church's proclamation of faith: "we believe in". The confession "we believe in" articulates not only the trust of individuals in God's grace, but it also affirms the trust of the whole Church in God. There is a bond of communion among those who join together in making a common confession of their faith. However, as long as the churches which confess the Creed are not united with one another, the visible communion of the one, holy, catholic and apostolic Church remains impaired.

4. Just as in baptism the confession of faith is made in response to God's grace, so too the Church's on-going confession is made in response to God's grace and love, most particularly vouchsafed in the preached

word and celebrated sacraments of the Church. Hence the Church's liturgy is the proper context for the Church's confession of faith.

5. Faith, which finds expression in the confession of the Creed, is a gift of God through the Holy Spirit. It involves the free submission of the believer, complete confidence and trust, waiting for God's help in reliance upon the testimonies which God has given of his love in creation, in redemption and in sanctification.

Commentary

In the West Augustine pointed to three aspects of the act of believing: to believe that God exists *(credere Deum)*, to believe God *(credere Deo)* and to believe in God *(credere in Deum)*. "Believing in" encompasses the first two, but goes beyond them and involves the personal commitment of completely entrusting oneself to God. This is also evident in the Apostles' Creed which uses "credere in" only in relation to the three persons of the Trinity and not with reference to the Church. The Nicene Creed, however, uses "believe in" also with reference to the Church. In Greek *pisteuomen eis* has a broader meaning indicating simply the object intended in the act of belief.

PART I

We Believe in One God

A. THE ONE GOD

6. Christians *believe* that "the One true God", who made himself known to Israel, has revealed himself supremely in the "one whom he has sent", namely Jesus Christ (John 17:3);[1] that, in Christ, God has reconciled the world to himself (2 Cor. 5:19); and that, by his Holy Spirit, God brings new and eternal life to all who through Christ put their trust in him.

7. This faith in a single, universal God who is Creator, Redeemer and Sustainer of everything is *challenged* by those who doubt whether there is any reality beyond the visible world, providing the source of its being and continuing life: for them a conception of God is no more than an expression and projection of human wishes and fears. Even when it is acknowledged that there are powers transcending the visible reality of the world the question is, can it be maintained that there is only one such power and should that power be conceived as purely transcendent or also as immanent in the world, and how can these aspects be reconciled?

8. Many who agree with Christians in a belief in one God find the Trinitarian affirmation of Christians difficult to understand. For Jews and Muslims particularly, the Christian concept of the Triune God has been a stumbling block because it seems to deny monotheism. There are also Christians today who consider that the Christian doctrine of the Trinity at the very least requires fresh interpretation and even linguistic revision. Moreover, there is widespread neglect and misunderstanding of the doctrine. It is sometimes explained "modalistically", as if it meant that God is really one, but because of human limitations is understood in three

---

[1] Bible passages are quoted from the *Revised Standard Version*.

different ways, or "tri-theistically", as though worship of God the Father, God the Son and God the Holy Spirit were three separable and different kinds of worship. Many feel that the traditional Trinitarian teaching is too speculative in comparison with the biblical language about God the Father, the Son and the Holy Spirit. Such challenges ask for contemporary work of clarification.

I. The Creed and its biblical witness

a) The text of the Creed
   9. "We believe in one God."

   (AC : "I believe in God")[2]

10. The Nicene Creed begins with confessing belief in one God. The theme of the oneness of God is in turn expanded in the three articles of the Creed in a Trinitarian way. The first article stresses belief in One God, the Father; the second, in One Lord, the Son of the Father; and the third, in the Holy Spirit, the Lord, who proceeds from the Father. Thus the One God is understood in terms of the Father, the Son and the Holy Spirit, the Father being the source of all divinity. Corresponding to the oneness of the Triune God, the Creed affirms that there is also only one Church and one baptism (cf. Eph. 4:4-6). Thus the Creed emphasizes oneness in all the three articles.

> *Commentary*
>   From their Jewish heritage Christians have known from the beginning that "there is no God but one". The Church of the second century affirmed against Marcion the unity of the God who creates and redeems. It took time before the Church gave a fully reasoned and well articulated account of the relation between the "one God, the Father, from whom are all things and for whom we exist" and the "one Lord, Jesus Christ, through whom are all things and through whom we exist" (1 Cor. 8:6). The decisive moment came with the Arian controversy. The Council of Nicea (325) affirmed the Son to be "from the substance of the Father" *(ek tes ousias tou Patros)* and "consubstantial with the Father" *(homoousios to Patri).* After the subsequent controversy of Pneumatomachianism, the Council of Constantinople (381) also declared the Lordship of the Holy Spirit "who proceeds from the

---

[2] AC = Apostles' Creed.

Father and who with the Father and the Son is worshipped and glorified". In all this the Church had no intention of putting the unity of God into question; rather, the One God was understood as Triune on the basis of his redemptive activity in history. Baptism continued to take place in the single name of the Father, the Son and the Holy Spirit.

In subsequent centuries different interpretations were advanced concerning the ultimate principle of unity in the Trinity, namely, whether this was to be found in the divine being *(ousia)* or in the person *(hypostasis)* of the Father or in the inter-relatedness and mutual indwelling of the three persons in their communion with one another. However, both East and West have always confessed in worship the unity of God and the distinction of persons with equal insistence; and it is in worship that the personal character of the Triune God is most apparent.

On the whole, Nicene theology stressed at the same time the uniqueness of each of the three persons *(hypostases)* in the one God revealed throughout the history of salvation, *and* their unity in communion *(koinonia)* in the one divine being. Today care needs to be taken with such words as "substance" (which now often suggests material entities, subject to instrumental measurement), "essence" (which may recall the language of a discredited metaphysics) or "person" (which could be interpreted as referring to some isolated individual centre of consciousness). Contemporary Trinitarian theology continues to discuss, and even more so than in some earlier periods, how the oneness of God together with the three "persons" can be appropriately expressed. There is agreement, however, that an adequate and exhaustive rational account of the mystery of the Triune God celebrated in the liturgy of the Church remains beyond human comprehension. Trinitarian doctrine and its language can only give the reasons for confessing the three persons as well as the one God.

b) Biblical witness

11. In the course of its history *Israel* came to believe in the uniqueness of God. This finds its classical expression in the "Shema Israel": "Hear, O Israel, the LORD is our God, the LORD alone. You shall love the LORD your God with all your heart, and with all your soul, and with all your might" (Deut. 6:4f.) It is most emphatically expounded in the prophecies of Second Isaiah where the LORD, the Creator and Redeemer, is confes-

sed explicitly as the only God, not only for Israel, but for all peoples. Other gods are mere idols: "And there is no other god besides me, a righteous God and a Saviour; there is none besides me. Turn to me and be saved, all the ends of the earth! For I am God, and there is no other" (Isa. 45:21-22).

12. The Old Testament emphasis on the uniqueness of God was continued in the *New Testament*. Jesus affirmed the faith of Israel concerning the one God. He dismissed Satan by citing the Scriptures: "You shall worship the LORD your God, and him only shall you serve" (Matt. 4:10; cf. Deut. 6:13). He endorsed the "Hear, O Israel" as the first and great commandment and the way to eternal life (Mark 12:29; Matt. 22:37; Luke 10:27).

13. However, the New Testament also makes clear that this God is in a unique relationship with Jesus Christ. Jesus is called his Son (Luke 1:32-33; Mark 1:11 pars.). Jesus addresses this God as "Father", using the intimate word "Abba" (Mark 14:36). Jesus is the Father's own beloved and only Son (John 1:18; 3:16; Rom. 8:32; Col. 1:13). Whoever has seen the Son has seen the Father (John 14:9), for the Father and the Son are "one" (John 10:30; 17:11). While remaining distinct, the Father and the Son "dwell" in each other (John 17:21).

14. At the same time the New Testament also links the Spirit — "who proceeds from the Father" (John 15:26) — with the Son (cf. para. 210). According to the prayer of Christ, the Father sends the Holy Spirit into the world, "the other Paraclete", the Spirit who "makes alive" and guides into all the truth (John 16:7). All three, Father, Son and Holy Spirit, are named together in the early apostolic preaching and writing (2 Cor. 13:13; Eph. 4:4-6).

II. Explication for today

The One God: Father, Son and Spirit

15. The particularity of Christian faith in the one God is based on the revelation of Father, Son and Holy Spirit. Therefore, the divine "*economy*", the history of salvation in creation, reconciliation and eschatological fulfilment, is at the basis of the Trinitarian faith. On the other hand, the One God is in all eternity the Father, the Son, and the Holy Spirit. Economic and eternal Trinity is but one reality. The two aspects are inseparable from each other. This unity of economic and eternal Trinity has not always been duly taken into consideration. But it is only on the basis of the historical revelation of God in Jesus Christ that the

Trinitarian faith of the Church can be accounted for. The Trinitarian doctrine is not a product of abstract speculation, but a summary of how God is revealed in Jesus Christ.

16. It is in the *divine economy* that the separation and alienation of the world from God as a result of sin and evil is overcome through the reconciling work of the Son and the transfiguring presence of the Spirit. In the mystery of this divine economy of salvation the one God is revealed as life and love communicating himself to his creatures. God the *Father* reconciles the world to himself through the incarnation, the ministry and suffering of his eternal Son. In the *Son* God shares the human condition even to death, in order to offer to humanity forgiveness of sin, resurrection and eternal life (John 3:16). Through the *Spirit* God raised the crucified one to a new and imperishable life that will bring about the final transfiguration and glorification of our lives and of the whole creation in the eschatological future. By the proclamation of this good news the Spirit even now kindles faith, love and hope in the hearts of those who receive the gospel, as even before the incarnation of the Son he encouraged the hope for the future salvation of humanity.

17. The *incarnate Son* reveals that in God's eternal glory, before all time and history, his divine life is mutual self-giving and communion, that "God is love" (1 John 4:8). This eternal love and communion between Father and Son is revealed in the cross of Christ and in his resurrection through the power of the Spirit. Cross and resurrection cannot be understood apart from the Trinitarian communion of Father, Son and Spirit, nor can the Trinity be understood apart from the cross and the resurrection. The cross is the affirmation of a love which is stronger than sin and death, and the resurrection confirms that this divine love is indeed and will be victorious.

18. The eternal source of that living Trinitarian communion of love is *God the Father*. But the Father was never without the Son, nor was he ever without his Spirit. The mutual indwelling of the three persons is the seal of their unity. God's eternal life and glory is in the free giving of the persons in mutual communion to each other. The divine unity originates from the Father as its source, but is maintained in the obedience of the Son and in the testimony of the Spirit glorifying the Son in the Father and the Father in the Son.

Commentary

Often there is too little awareness of the Trinitarian character of the divine unity itself, as the Christian faith professes it. Frequently the one God is simply identified with the Father, while the Son and the Spirit are either ontologically subordinated to him or imagined as mere modes of the revelation of the Father. In distinction from this, the mutuality of inter-relations among the three persons in maintaining the "monarchy" of the Father should be understood to be the concrete form of divine unity.

19. The Church believes in this eternal communion of love, as it is revealed and actualized in the divine economy: it is at work in the creation of the world as well as in its redemption and in its sanctification and ultimate glorification. Although the work of creation is attributed specifically to the Father, the work of redemption to the Son, and the work of sanctification and glorification to the Spirit, the work of each of the Trinitarian persons implies the presence and co-operation of all three. Thus God is one. None of the three persons of the Trinity has a life of his own apart from the others.

20. The Triune God is the ground of unity as well as diversity in his creation. The Trinity can be seen as the model of a diversity that does not destroy unity and of a unity that does not suffocate diversity for the sake of uniformity. Therefore, the one God can be creatively present in the multitude of his creatures.

21. The tendency to identify God and nature, especially marked in philosophical forms of pantheism since the seventeenth century, rejects the idea of a purely transcendent God who could not be present in the created world. But the Triune God of the Christian faith is at the same time transcendent and yet present in his creation that originates through his Logos and Spirit. The Triune God is present in the depth of our existence, in spite of our alienation from our Creator. This creative, sustaining and saving presence of God does not destroy the creature's freedom, but on the contrary enables it to enjoy this creaturely independence, to actively preserve it and to engage in acts of devotion to others and to God. But such independence also includes the risk of alienation from the Creator.

22. The infinite God also remains transcendent over his creation, dwelling in an unattainable light. In this transcendance, God is the source of newness in his creation, urging it towards a final fulfilment of created existence in communion with God and among the creatures themselves. But even in their eschatological glorification, the creatures will never be absorbed into God. Our acceptance of our difference from God remains the condition of communion with him in praising him as Creator and

Redeemer of his creation. Therefore, the belief that God will be all in all (1 Cor. 15:28) does not entail pantheism.

Challenges posed by atheism and secularism

23. Faith in one God is challenged by various forms of *atheism*. There are atheists who affirm that belief in God, far from being *the* way of life and salvation, constitutes a threat to the freedom and dignity of humankind; in this case, belief in God is seen as an illusion arising from psychological, ideological, sociological or even economic grounds. Others see in the results of the natural sciences and logical positivism reasons to deny the existence of God, because it seems unnecessary in explaining the world. Even within churches there are persons who confess Christ, but succumb to the atmosphere of diffidence created by these powerful arguments and deny the existence of God. Others are not able to reconcile the evil in the world with faith in the Creator God (which is the problem of theodicy). Many people, confronted with the problem of surviving in our world today, are unable to find any divine or religious frame of reference for life. As a result, some of them turn to utopianism or nihilism. Finally, many people are purely indifferent (practical atheism). In faithfulness to the gospel, Christians should listen carefully to challenges of the particular forms of atheism in their contexts, and in that light be prepared to scrutinize the adequacy of their conceptions of God and of God's relation to the world. This especially applies where the atheism in question has at least in part been a reaction to distorted forms of Christian doctrine and life.

24. Christian reactions to the different forms of atheism cannot be confined to a theoretical level. Atheism also involves the question of life-orientation. Christian faith in God fundamentally means taking up a new life in the light of the God who has been revealed in Jesus Christ, while, according to the Gospel of John, those who persist in a sinful life show that in fact they refuse faith in God (cf. 3:20). Rational argument is not the only, perhaps not even the most important, feature in the presentation of the faith to others. Crucial is the convincing witness of one's own life, for example through the overcoming of tragedy or through an inner richness of life which comes from faith.

25. Nevertheless, there are also arguments against various forms of atheism. First, concerning the claim that the scientific explanation of the world is sufficient, it should be pointed out that that explanation is in fact never complete. It does not fulfil the same function as the interpretation of the world in terms of creation does, which relates to the

meaning of the world as a whole, but on a different level from science.

26. Second, in response to those who find it impossible to reconcile faith in a Creator God with the experience of unnecessary suffering and evil in the world, we must acknowledge that here human thought comes up against the limits of what can be explained. This painful awareness has become particularly acute under the pressure of contemporary experiences. Christian response to that challenge is the faith that in the cross of Christ God has shared human suffering and death, and by this solidarity has opened to us the way to overcome despair (cf. paras 60-61). This is, of course, no "solution" to the problem of evil, but it enables Christians to cope with it.

27. Third, particularly powerful forms of atheistic arguments in modern times have been the various claims at explaining religion as a product of illusory projections. But this type of argument presupposes a view of human nature without religion as an essential ingredient. That is not in accordance with the facts of cultural history where, from the earliest times, religion was a constitutive factor, and the assumption of non-religious men and women producing religion cannot be sustained.

Commentary

While the religious traditions of humankind are indeed all testimonies of human experience and thought, they support the fact that human nature is inescapably religious. This means that to be fully human includes a religious dimension of life. This is not necessarily expressed in the language of "religion" in the specific sense. It may consist in the awareness of some ultimate reality, or it may be implicit in the form of ideological claims and commitments.

It is in religions, in the specific sense of the word, on the basis of some experience of divine reality, that this human condition becomes explicit. Religions are not unnecessary inventions of beings whose primordial nature could be adequately described in purely secular terms as some atheists assume.

The religious dimension belongs to the roots of the distinctively human condition: so the fullness of being human is missed where the awareness of a reality transcending everything finite is obscured or extinguished. Instead human fullness is promised whenever this transcending reality is taken seriously and sought after as a source of possible answers and solutions to the promises, inadequacies and perversions of human life.

28. Closely related to the atheism that arises from the apparent self-sufficiency of secular science in describing the world is the secularism of modern societies. It affirms the self-sufficiency of the social and cultural system that relegates religion to the status of a merely private affair and denies any accountability of the public order to God. Secularism must not be confused with secularity and secularization. Secularity of the social and political order in distinction from the Church developed in the history of Christian culture to a far greater degree than in other cultural systems. The affirmation of a relative autonomy of the secular world is part of the historical contribution of Christianity and can be understood as a consequence of biblical monotheism on the one hand and the provisional status of the present world and its social and natural order on the other. When in Genesis 1 the sun, the moon and the stars (in contrast to the belief of some ancient religions) are no longer divine beings, but creatures fashioned by the One God, the result is a secularization of nature. When in early Christianity the present social order was denied ultimate value, it was in some way secularized. But it was not cut loose from any relation to the ultimate reality of God. This separation, however, constitutes the secularism of modern society. Such a secularism is a problem not only in Europe and North America, but affects through the spread of modernization (industrialization plus bureaucratic administration) countries in all parts of the world.

29. The world of finite things and the secular social system both lack ultimate meaning and purpose without a transcendent reality as their basis. Throughout history men and women of every race and culture have found the basis for their existence and for the meaning of their life in the certitude of the existence and action of God. Wherever this is the case, God is the source of moral values, so that his voice is heard in the human conscience. Moreover belief in God is a source of hope in the face of death, suffering, failure and strife, a hope surpassing everything that can be achieved by human efforts, but also inspiring efforts at creating at least provisional forms of justice and of sustainable social order and conditions that allow for a life of human dignity.

30. In secular societies the experience of meaninglessness produces various reactions. Some of them have taken the form of new religious movements often connected with some allusion to modern scientific approaches. Besides, there are many forms of superstition, even satanism. Furthermore, various religious groups make missionary efforts to take advantage of this situation. This new religiosity is in special danger of producing what has been called "false gods", mere projections

from the desires and anxieties of human hearts. But the forging of false gods and the corresponding idolatry is by no means confined to the new religiosity. It occurs wherever finite things are turned into objects of ultimate trust and worship (see Rom. 1:23; Phil. 3:19). It pervades or at least tempts people in all religions, but also occurs in other than explicitly religious forms, because whatever becomes an object of ultimate trust (e.g. possessions, power, honour) functions as an idol in the place of the true God. Secularism as such (like other ideologies) involves elements of idolatry, when the secular world is absolutized. Yet what is wrong in secularism cannot be overcome by projected religion, but only by turning to the transcendent reality that is prior to all human knowledge and action.

Challenges posed by other religions and living faiths

31. In the early centuries Christians believing in one God seemed to stand apart from *other religions*. However a closer look at the apologetic works of the early Christians shows that Christian theology shared some common ground not only with Judaism, but also with other religions, especially with religious Hellenistic philosophy. The early Christian attitude, echoing St Peter's words in Acts 10:34f., is especially important today in view of the developing dialogue between Christianity and Judaism, or Christianity and other religions, especially Islam.

32. In explicating the Trinitarian confession of the One God, Christians are confronted with the fact that other monotheistic religions do not share their faith in a Triune God though all agree in believing in the One God of Abraham. Indeed, Christians are often accused either of idolatry (Judaism) or polytheism (Islam). But *Jewish* tradition itself knows of realities that represent the transcendent God within this world — his *Name*, *Glory*, *Shechinah*, *Tora* and *Wisdom*. Do these realities, which are distinguished from God's transcendent being, really represent the presence of God himself? In that case the distinction between transcendence and immanence, which is implicit in the origins of the Christian Trinitarian doctrine, also applies to the Jewish conception of the One God. Indeed a transcendent God who could not be present in this world would hardly be the God of the Old Testament prophets. The Christian belief in the Trinitarian God, however, explicitly asserts the unity of God as a differentiated unity.

33. With regard to the *Islamic* charge of polytheism, it is important to stress that the Christian faith never intended to surrender the oneness of God. Nor did the Trinitarian doctrine of the Church intend to limit or to

weaken the affirmation of the unity of God. Rather, the Trinitarian differentiation of the unity of God is a condition of a truly consistent monotheism because it does not leave the principle of plurality and diversity outside of that unity so that unity would be a mere correlate to a plurality that was not included in the divine life.

34. In *other religions*, e.g. African and Asian traditional religions, Buddhism or Hinduism, the manifoldness of divinity is experienced in human beings and animals as well as in plants and things. These religions challenge the Christian Trinitarian belief as being too abstract and cut off from the realities of day-to-day life. In some way this challenge also comes from the affirmation of manifold manifestations of divine reality by some Hindus and Buddhists. Furthermore, syncretistic movements gain ground in a number of countries traditionally informed by the influence of the Christian faith. These movements often function as compensation for the Christian Trinitarian faith which is no longer understood in its fullness, richness and concreteness. In the face of these challenges Christians believe that the concreteness of the One God is no other than in the work of the Father, the Son and the Holy Spirit.

35. Although Christians confess God, revealed to them in Jesus Christ, in a way which, according to their conviction, is the only true way, they do not deny important elements of truth in other religions. This commits Christians to an attitude of respect and an openness for dialogue, and "churches should seek ways in which Christian communities can enter into dialogue with their neighbours of different faiths and ideologies.... Dialogues should normally be planned together.... Partners in dialogues should take stock of the religious, cultural and ideological diversity of their local situation.... Partners in dialogue should be free to 'define themselves'.... Dialogue should generate educational efforts in the community....".[3]

B. THE FATHER ALMIGHTY

36. Christians confess the one God as "Father Almighty". Thus they affirm their confidence that their life and death are embraced by the parental care of a God whose love has come into this world in his Son Jesus Christ and remains with us in the communion of the Holy Spirit. To call this loving and faithful God at the same time "almighty" points to the

---

[3] Cf. *Guidelines on Dialogue with People of Living Faiths and Ideologies*, WCC, Geneva, 1979, pp. 17-19.

assurance that all life, reality and history are not left to themselves or to worldly powers and principalities, but are grounded in and sustained by a God whose power is as unlimited as his love.

37. Today these affirmations are *challenged* even among Christians. According to widespread popular opinion the fatherhood of God has been taken to imply that God is male and masculine and that patriarchal and authoritarian features are characteristic of God. Therefore, men have been assumed to be more in the image of God than women and patriarchy and authoritarianism are suspected as being woven into the very fabric of the churches' life. Further, the confession of God's almightiness seems to reduce human beings to slaves of a distant, unreachable authority. In the face of evil, sin, injustice, suffering and death and the "powers" at work in this world there is seen to be a contradiction between the affirmation of God's love and God's almightiness.

I. The Creed and its biblical witness

a) The text of the Creed

38. "We believe in... the Father, the Almighty."

(AC: "I believe in... the Father almighty")

39. The Creed goes on to identify the One God more particularly as "Father Almighty". Much else that might also be affirmed concerning the nature and being of God such as eternity, wisdom, goodness, faithfulness is not explicitly stated. "Father Almighty" is the Creed's first qualification of "One God". It leads on to the following words: "maker of heaven and earth ...", which further draw out one main dimension of its meaning. In the first article Father and Creator are held together in a particular way. Concerning creation, it is said of the Son: "through" him "all things were made"; of the Holy Spirit: he is "the Lord, the Giver of life"; but "Creator" is confessed primarily of the Father.

40. "Father almighty" may be understood in two ways according to whether "Almighty" is treated as a substantive in apposition to "Father" ("the Father, the Almighty") or as an adjective ("the Father almighty"). Both interpretations have been common in the history of the Church. The first stresses the distinct meaning of "Father" and "Almighty"; the second stresses their conjunction, in particular the qualification of "Father" by "Almighty" and "Almighty" by "Father".

41. In the time of the early Church there were many claimants to universal sovereignty: the Hellenistic pantheon; deterministic fate; the

Platonic forms; Aristotle's unmoved mover; the impersonal world-reason of the Stoic philosophy; the esoteric teachings and rituals of the mystery religions; the Gnostic aeons; or even — not least — the apotheosis of earthly dominion in the Roman imperial cult. Against all of these the Church and the Creed affirmed: the Father of Jesus Christ, and none other, is *Pantokrator*.

42. In the fourth century, the wording and content of the first article were not controversial. Nevertheless, in earlier conflicts with Gnosticism, which drew a radical distinction between the Father of Jesus Christ and the Creator or cause of this material universe, they had to be defended. Against such opposition, the proclamation of the "One God", "Father", "the Almighty" as "the maker of heaven and earth" was successfully upheld. It is in this setting that the particular force of the inclusion of Pantokrator in the Creed is to be understood.

b) Biblical witness
"Father"

43. The Father-Son image came to be used in the Old Testament to characterize the relation between the LORD and the people of God. Because the LORD created and established Israel, the LORD is Israel's father (Deut. 32:6). This fatherhood is one of loving care and compassion (Hos. 11:1f.; Jer. 3:19). Many of the qualities associated with it include those often designated as "feminine". This is further supported by motherhood images. The LORD is likened to a midwife (Ps. 22:9), a suckling mother (Isa. 49:15), a mother comforting her child (Isa. 66:13). Nevertheless the LORD is never addressed as "Mother".

44. Central to the New Testament is the fatherhood of God. At the end of his life, in Gethsemane, Jesus cries "Abba, Father" (Mark 14:36 and parallels) and, finally, on the cross, commends himself into his Father's hands (Luke 23:46). This relation to the One Jesus called his Father occurs in the infancy narratives, in the messianic declaration at his baptism, and in the mode of his preaching and prayer. In the language of John, "Father" is not simply one among many images but the special and characteristic way in which Jesus addresses God. Particularly in prayer Jesus addresses God as Father, sometimes using Abba, thus evoking a close familial relationship. So close is this relationship between Jesus and his Father that he says to Philip: "He who has seen me has seen the Father" (John 14:9). The Father is most fully known as a Father loving the world, in the giving of his Son, in the cross and resurrection (John 3:16).

45. In the Gospels, Jesus urges his disciples also to address God as "Our Father". According to Paul, God is "our Father" because he is the Father of Jesus who graciously allows us to share by adoption in his unique Father-Son relationship. The Spirit who unites us with the Son sets us free as brothers and sisters to call God "Abba". This intimate, familial relationship with the Father is for all human beings without any differentiation (cf. Rom. 8:14-15; Gal. 4:6). According to Jesus, God's fatherly care extends to other creatures as well (Matt. 6:26; cf. also 1 Cor. 8:6).

Almighty (Pantokrator)

46. With regard to God being Pantokrator, in many instances the Old Testament testifies to the LORD's power, to his might witnessed in victory over enemies and over the forms of chaos, and manifested in the ordering of creation (Ps. 93). This power will be witnessed in the final triumph over his enemies and in the dawning of the new age (Isa. 9:6). The Old Testament never speaks of an abstract omnipotence, always of God's power manifested in action.

47. In the New Testament Pantokrator occurs only a few times, all but one in the Apocalypse. Characteristic is Rev. 1:8: "I am the Alpha and the Omega, says the Lord God, who is and who was and who is to come, the Pantokrator". The affirmation has both a clear liturgical ring and an apocalyptic colour. It is a solemn, expectant and jubilant cry of praise and hope in the midst of a dark and profoundly ambiguous world, a world which appears to be in the hands of Antichrist.

In the single New Testament passage outside the Apocalypse in which Pantokrator is used — 2 Cor. 6:16-18 — the same confident trust is expressed. Having praised the faithfulness and calling of God it ends: "and I will be a father to you, and you shall be my sons and daughters, says the Lord Pantokrator" (v. 18). The authentic sense of the Father as Pantokrator is thus manifested in the New Testament. It is *doxological* and *eschatological*. It testifies to the faithfulness and ultimate sovereignty of God as the ground of faith, confidence and trust.

48. The affirmation of God almighty has an even deeper foundation in the New Testament. This foundation discloses the nature and quality of God's sovereign power. It is a power so transcendent that God could, in the incarnation, enter into his own creation and thereby victoriously assert his claim upon it through what appeared to be the absolute and final negation of his power, the crucifixion of the incarnate Son. The crucified Christ is "the power of God and the wisdom of God. The foolishness of God is wiser than men, and the weakness of God is stronger than men"

(1 Cor. 1:24-25). And in Christ's resurrection God reveals his power over sin and death. This is the sense in which God is Pantokrator, the one who holds all things, in whose hands the world and its destiny are securely grasped in spite of the reality of evil, sin, suffering and death. This creating, recreating and saving almightiness will be revealed to all in its fullness at the end of time when all things are brought to perfection in Christ.

II. Explication for today

The Father
The image of fatherhood and Father as a personal name

49. In the Creed the One God is confessed first as the Father. The Father is the source of all divinity; the second article confesses further how this Father is the Father of the unique Son, and finally the third article shows that this Father is the one from whom the Holy Spirit proceeds. Thus the fatherhood of God must be understood in connection with the unique Son and with the Holy Spirit.

When the Creed uses "begotten" to describe the eternal relation of the Father to the Son, it is concerned with the relation of origin. Here, as in the biblical witness, the language does not imply biological fatherhood; it transcends the sexual distinction between male and female which had been part of the polytheistic conceptions of gods and goddesses in Israel's cultural surroundings.

Because the human mind can never comprehend fully the nature and being of the transcendent God, Christians are always obliged, when speaking of God, to use language, symbols and images, knowing that these are only partial and approximate ways to describe God. This is supremely true when speaking of the inner life, origin and relationships of the persons of the Trinity. Words of human experience which express truths about the origin of God are not meant to imply any sexual connotation. Such words enable the Church to confess that in God the life of the Son originates in the Father.

Some patristic writers express the same origin in other ways such as the source and the river, the sun and its rays, the principle and its derivatives. In these images the sexual connotation is absent but something vitally important is missing: the personal relationship.

50. We may not surrender the language of "Father" for it is the way in which Jesus addressed, and spoke of, God and how Jesus taught his disciples to address God. It is in relation to the use of Father by Christ

Jesus himself that the Church came to believe in Jesus as the Son of God. The language of "Father" and "Son" links the Christian community through the ages and binds it in a communion of faith. Moreover, it is the language which expresses the personal relationships within the inner life of the Trinity, and in our own relations with God.

51. Nevertheless, the Church must make clear that this language neither attributes biological maleness to God nor implies that what we call "masculine" qualities, assigned only to men, are the only characteristics belonging to God. Jesus uses only some of the characteristics of human fatherhood in speaking of God. He also uses other characteristics than those of human fatherhood. Indeed, God embraces, fulfils and transcends all that we know concerning human persons, both male or female, and human characteristics whether masculine or feminine. However, "Father" is not simply one amongst a number of metaphors or images used to describe God. It is the distinctive term addressed by Jesus himself to God.

52. We may not surrender the names Father and Son. They are rooted in Jesus' intimate relation to the God whom he proclaimed, though he also used other characteristics than those relating to human nature. Beyond his own language, however, Christian language about God also draws from the resources of the whole biblical tradition. There we find "feminine" images too in talking about God. We must become more attentive to these.[4] This will affect our understanding of the relationships between men and women created in God's image and the ordering and working of the structures of the Church and society called to bear witness to wholeness.

> *Commentary*
>
> In some churches and cultural contexts there is an ongoing debate over whether God may also be addressed as "Our Mother". In this discussion the distinction between image and name is important.

Scope of God's fatherhood

53. The fatherhood of God relates in the first place to Jesus of Nazareth who is the *Son*. The fatherhood of God is understood in the way Jesus related to God and spoke of God as his Father in obedient acceptance of his suffering and mission. God is in all eternity the same as he is revealed in the history of the incarnate Son Jesus. Eternal fatherhood implies eternal Sonship. The person of the eternal Son became incarnate in Jesus of Nazareth.

---

[4] Cf. para. 43.

54. God is also the Father of the *community of all those who recognize his lordship*: the people of Israel and in a distinct, though related, way Christians. The Father calls his children to a life of love and obedience. In doing this he is not the coercive, authoritarian, domineering Father who holds his children to him by force. He allows them space and freedom to become what he wills them to be. He also disciplines his children in love and mercy as they grow, through the power of the Spirit, into the full stature of sons and daughters of their heavenly Father.

55. Through the Spirit *Christians* partake in the life of the crucified and risen Son and are therefore entitled to address God as their Father, Abba, as Jesus did (Rom. 8:14-17). In, with and through him they intercede for each other and for the world. As children of God they share in the relation of the Son to the Father. They are made brothers and sisters of the Son through incorporation by baptism into the death and resurrection of Christ Jesus. As the Son's obedience was even unto death, so Christians are called to follow that same way, knowing that as in fatherly love God raised the Son from death, so in the same love the Father wills to give eternal life to all the baptized.

56. God, as creator and sustainer, is also the Father of *all beings* (1 Cor. 8:6). Through the Son and through the Spirit, the providence of the Father extends to all creatures and aims at re-uniting them in the community of the kingdom. This universal scope of God's fatherhood implies that Christians are called to share with, and care for, their brothers and sisters whether they are regarded as friends or enemies — within the human family in their joys and sufferings.

The Almighty

57. The close association of Creator and Almighty with Father in the opening statement of the Creed underlines the idea that authority and dominion belong to the fatherhood of God. The Father God is the one who rules and wields authority over all creation, "the Almighty". The term used in the Creed is Pantokrator, literally "the one who holds and governs all things". It does not mean "one who can do anything he wants" in an unqualified way, but rather "one in whose hands all things are". It is less a description of absolute omnipotence than of universal providence. To call the Father Pantokrator is to affirm that the whole universe is in his grasp, that he does not, and will not, let it go. At the same time it brings with it (at least in principle) the de-throning of all other claimants to

universal sovereignty, to government and mastery over the world and its history and destiny.

58. The Church confesses the unlimited power of God to carry through his gracious and merciful purposes for humanity, and for the world; to bring about their consummation in the kingdom in a new creation, in a new heaven and a new earth. Faith in God's omnipotence gives confidence that "the powers of the present age" — whether political, economic, scientific, industrial, military, ideological or indeed religious — do not control and will not have the last word concerning the destiny of the world and humankind. The Lordship of the Almighty relativizes and judges them all: it confronts all other claims to sovereignty, it is a challenge to every form of enslaving bondage. To confess the Lordship of the Almighty is to celebrate the liberating strength of the Creator and to proclaim hope for each individual and for the whole universe. The Church affirms and proclaims this faith against all appearances to the contrary.

59. The confession of God's omnipotence does not mean that he is to be conceived as a coercive and all-powerful tyrant. Rather, God's power is the power of creative love and of loving concern for creatures. It is expressed in God's patience in waiting for them to respond to that love and in readiness to endure revolt against his authority and to save them from the consequences of it. God does not over-ride the independent actions of his creatures, but God's judgments are inescapable if the sinner does not repent. The sinner has to bear the consequences of sin (Rom. 1:18ff.) which finally lead to death. However, the love of the Father as expressed in the sending of the Son to reconcile and redeem the world aims at preventing human sinfulness from destroying God's creation.

Omnipotence and theodicy

60. The confession of God's omnipotence must meet the doubts of those who cannot believe that the present world, shaken by natural catastrophies, full of injustice, hatred, envy, selfishness and suffering, could be the product of a God who is at the same time benevolent and almighty. How could God allow the powers of evil to prevail and to inflict unspeakable suffering upon the innocent?[5] This is one of the strongest justifications advanced for atheism, an atheism of moral protest against the condition of the world as we experience it.

---

[5] See also paras 26, 82 and 154ff.

61. Christian tradition argued that evil is a consequence of the freedom that is God's gift to human beings. But this does not provide a full answer to the question of theodicy, for evil is also present outside the realm of human responsibility. The ultimate answer lies in God's overcoming evil, suffering, and death in the reconciliation of the world through the Son of God. He took upon himself the suffering of the world. Only in his victory over the powers of sin and death, which will be complete in the world to come, when all tears will be wiped away (Rev. 21:4), will creation be finally reconciled to the Creator. This is the Christian hope. Meanwhile the sufferings and injustices of the present world ought not to obscure the fact that God is the ultimate power to be invoked against the powers of evil. This gives to those who believe in God the courage and hope they need to do all they can in struggling against such powers.

The Father Almighty

62. To sum up what has been said above, the terms "Father" and "Almighty" qualify each other. To speak only of the Father, forgetting that he is almighty, risks trivializing and sentimentalizing the divine fatherhood; to speak only of the Almighty, as if he were not also the Father, is to risk projecting a demonic vision of sheer arbitrary power. Only when the two aspects are held together, and their interpretation controlled by the revelation of their meaning in Jesus Christ, are these dangers guarded against.

C. THE CREATOR AND HIS CREATION

63. Christians believe that the world in which they live is not an autonomous entity, which has its origins, life and destiny in itself. Rather, they believe that the world is the work of God, the Creator, who called it into being out of nothing *(ex nihilo)* by his Word. God was not only the cause of its existence in the beginning, but is also the continuing source of its life and the final goal of its existence.

64. This affirmation is *challenged* because many today consider, under the influence of modern science, that the world is autonomous and self-sustaining, in need neither of a transcendent origin nor of a sustaining power. This world-view is connected with, though not a necessary consequence of, the rise of modern science. Another challenge comes to the Christian view of creation from the social reality of secularized

society in which religion seems superfluous as a factor of basic importance in the establishment and preservation of the social order.

65. A further challenge to the Christian view of creation comes from
those who, while believing that creation originated with God, hold that it
is now out of God's hands. Modern economic structures involve limitless
exploitation of natural resources and endanger the ecological balance of
life; nuclear weapons present a threat to the survival of humankind and
perhaps of the planetary systems, while genetic manipulation gives
people arbitrary control over God's creatures. In such ways, modern
scientific culture challenges the Christian belief that creation originated in
God, that it is continually sustained by him and governed according to the
purposes of his design, and the place of men and women in God's
creation as responsible stewards of his creation.

I. The Creed and its biblical witness

a) The text of the Creed

66. "We believe in one God...,
     maker of heaven and earth,
     of all that is, seen and unseen."

(AC : "I believe in God...,
     creator of heaven and earth.")

67. The Church inherited from the Old Testament the faith that God is
"the maker of heaven and earth, the visible and invisible world" (Gen.
1:1ff.; Col. 1:15f.), and like ancient Israel it had to face questions about
the goodness of God's creation and of the mystery of evil (2 Thess. 2:7)
in the world. In the first centuries after Christ the interpretation of
creation became again controversial when heretical teachings drove a
sharp wedge between the visible and invisible world, between matter and
spirit, the God of the Old Testament and of creation on the one hand and
the God and Father of Jesus Christ on the other, between Israel and the
Church, between the Old Testament writings and the New Testament
scriptures.

68. The Christian tradition taught that everything comes from God in
opposition to the view that the world was formed from pre-existent
matter — a belief expressed in various forms of Platonism. Against that,
early Christian theology argued that not only the form of matter but the
very existence of all comes from God *(ex nihilo)*. This excluded the idea
of the co-eternity of the cosmos and even the assumption of uncreated
matter.

b) Biblical witness

69. The Lord was understood as Creator from an early period. In the course of its history Israel came to proclaim the God of Israel as sovereign over all other powers. At the time of the Exile in Babylon, after the destruction of Jerusalem and the Temple, in the context of the struggle against the apparent humiliation and overthrow of the Lord by the Babylonians, Second Isaiah argued that Yahweh was the only God, the Creator and ruler of all. Not only did the Lord create the world by his word but through that same word God also directs the course of history (Isa. 55:11). Moreover, God's continuing care for the world, his acts of salvation in the history of the people, are interpreted as acts of re-creation. These acts will culminate in the eschatological act of salvation and re-creation (Isa. 51:10).

70. Israel's belief in creation finds its most extensive expression in Genesis 1 and 2. These chapters owe much to the religious traditions of the ancient Near East, especially to the Canaanites and the Babylonians. Although traces of belief in creation out of some existing matter can be detected behind the story, the Genesis account expressed Israel's own belief that God created by his word of command (Gen. 1). The Genesis account of creation can therefore be legitimately interpreted in terms of creation *ex nihilo* (2 Macc. 7:28; see also Rom. 4:17).

71. The Old Testament affirms that the whole universe has come into being through God and is dependent upon him as its maker (Gen. 1:1-2:25; Ps. 8; Isa. 40:25-26); the creation shows forth his wisdom and power (Ps. 104:24; Prov. 3:19-20); notwithstanding its inherent ambiguities, it bears witness to God's steadfast love and care (Ps. 136:4-9). The majesty of God, reflected in the creation, is a reason for worshipping and thanksgiving, for trusting and obeying God (Ps. 95; Isa. 40:27-31). Moreover, it is the Lord's continuing power that upholds and renews the creation (Ps. 104:25-30).

72. In the New Testament the *soteriological* and *eschatological* significance of creation comes to the fore in the context of the work of Jesus Christ and of the Holy Spirit: God who created in the beginning, creates anew and will create in the future (Mark 13:19; Eph. 2:10; Rev. 1:8). In the end God will be all in all (1 Cor. 15:28) and there will be "a new heaven and a new earth" (2 Pet. 3:13; Rev. 21:1; cf. Isa. 65:17; 66:22). All creatures and nature itself will be transformed and will participate in God's new world (Rom. 8:19-23).

73. In the New Testament the order of creation is seen to have its foundation in Jesus Christ (1 Cor. 8:6; John 1:1-18). God creates,

sustains, redeems and perfects his creation through Christ who is the centre of all that is (Col. 1:15-17; Eph. 1:9-10; Heb. 1:2-3). This divine economy, however, is not to be seen as continuous progress towards perfection but, rather, has to deal with the *destructive forces*, which result from sinful self-centredness and self-concern, the cause of evil and suffering in God's creation (Eph. 6:12). According to the New Testament the destructive forces finally lead to death in the individual and to the ultimate collapse of the created world. It is only God's sustaining and saving activity that counteracts and limits and will finally overcome the forces of evil at work in the world (1 Cor. 15:25-26). The Church, living under Christ as its head (Col. 1:18; Eph. 1:22-24) and having its members continuously transformed into the image of God's Son (Rom. 8:29; 1 Cor. 15:49), has a new vision of the ultimate purpose of the Creator and Redeemer, firmly believing in the future resurrection of the body and in the life of the world to come.

74. The belief in the creative power of God's word (Gen. 1; John 1:1-3; Heb. 11:3) and the confidence that God is able to create "out of nothing" (Rom. 4:17; Heb. 11:3; cf. Matt. 3:9) are characteristic of the Christian belief in God the Creator.

II. Explication for today

"Maker of heaven and earth, of all that is, seen and unseen"

75. The first article affirms that the one God, the Father, the Almighty, is also "the maker of heaven and earth, of all things visible and invisible". In the second article it is further clarified that the Son of the Father is the one "through whom all things came into existence". Finally the third article affirms that the Holy Spirit, who proceeds from the Father, is "the giver of life", and concludes with an eschatological reference to "the resurrection of the dead and the life of the world to come". In this way it is affirmed that the One God, the Father Almighty, is the *Creator* through the Son (Col. 1:16) and through the Holy Spirit (Ps. 104:30).

76. Faith in God the Creator implies that the *world* is the good creation of the Father and not an evil world hostile to him. Because the world is the gift of God, it is intrinsically good. Its God-given goodness is inherent in all creation whether seen or unseen, and holds together what is seen and unseen whether in the cosmos or in human beings. The Creed stresses that God is the Creator of both "heaven and earth and of all things visible and invisible". This means that the

created universe is not made up only of those material, tangible realities of the world. The dividing line between what is seen and unseen appears to be shifting in the process of human experience and scientific descriptions of the world of creation. But there will always be a difference between what we can grasp and what is beyond our grasp. Invisible (spiritual, subconscious and suprasensible) dimensions which belong to the wholeness of God's creation, according to the Creed, are also, just as the material world, a locus for both good and evil. Notwithstanding the distinction between the visible and the invisible aspects of creation, there is no dualism or separation between "material" and "spiritual" in the Christian understanding of the world, although Christian thought was sometimes tempted to acquiesce in popular dualism. The tension between the two belongs to our present condition of time but will be overcome in the realization of the eschatological vision (cf. 1 Cor. 13:12).

77. The contingency of individual existence as well as of the world, the precariousness and fragility of all life, remind the Christian of the complete *dependence* of finite reality on the power of God transcending every finite reality and order. This dependence affects every moment of human life and the continuing existence of the natural and social world and its order. It comprises both the origin of their existence and their preservation at any given time. The notion of *creatio ex nihilo* accordingly relates to both these aspects. For the Christian this strengthens the conviction of the goodness of creation.

Creation and the Triune God

78. The Trinitarian understanding of God is indispensable for a Christian understanding of God's relation to the world as creation. The One God both transcends and is present in his creation. Moreover each divine Person, Father, Son and Holy Spirit, of the one God participates in both this transcendence and this immanence. When Christians speak of God's works concerning creation in relation to the divine persons, they should always insist that the three persons fully participate in that work. Thus when they say that God the Father, the source of the Triune being (see para. 18), is the God above creation who "in the beginning" created out of nothing all that is, they remember that this work is accomplished through the Word, God's Son, and through the Holy Spirit, the *Creator Spiritus*. Likewise, when they speak of the incarnation of the divine Word who became flesh (cf. John 1:14), they also affirm that God the Father and Creator is thereby manifesting his

faithfulness to and in his creation. They affirm that — as in the beginning, so in the incarnation — the Spirit is active. He leads to completion the work of the Father and the Son, so that everything culminates in Christ, the first-born of all (Col. 1:15). Again, when they affirm the work of the Holy Spirit within creation, giving life, inspiring and empowering the creation towards the fulfilment of its destiny, they praise God the Father whose mysterious purpose embraces all things (cf. Eph. 1:9) and God the Son in whom all things visible and invisible hold together. It is always the one and the same Triune God who is active in all aspects of his work.

God's glory in creation

79. The creation is firm in its foundation, very good and magnificent, because it comes from God the Creator. It is not only made for use by humankind: God the Creator rejoices in his work (Gen. 1:31); all humankind shares in this joy and in some way perceives the eternal power and deity of God in his work (Rom. 1:20). Israel sees in the creation the characteristic features of God's *glory* on earth and in heaven (Ps. 8:2; Isa. 6:1-3). The Church affirms this presence of God's glory in the whole creation and rejoices in it with thanksgiving. This occurs particularly in the liturgy where, in fellowship with those who suffer, the Church celebrates the transfiguration and renewal by God himself of all creation, a renewal which will culminate in the kingdom.

80. All of this means that the entire creation, through the presence and activity of the Triune God in it, is full of his glory (Isa. 6:3) and in the end will be transformed by participation in God's glory (Rom. 8:21). Therefore, in Christian Trinitarian perception, creation is not to be seen in any sense as standing apart from God, as the deistic view asserts, nor confused with God, as the pantheistic view claims.[6] Rather, creation though other than God, and still "in bondage to decay and groaning in travail" (Rom. 8:21-22), can be properly understood only in relation to God as its Creator, Redeemer and Sustainer.

God sustains and governs his world

81. In his providence God cares for his creation. He responds to the need of each creature for sustained existence which arises every day anew. God did not create the cosmos once in the beginning and then leave it to itself. Rather, through his continuous creation God preserves and sustains his creation at every moment.

---

[6] See para. 21.

82. The Church recognizes that the goodness and wholeness of creation is constantly threatened by death and decay, natural catastrophes and manifold sufferings of created beings. Thus the whole history of creation is marked by a certain ambiguity which seems to be characteristic of this world as it is known in daily experience (see paras 60-61). Nevertheless, because of the redemptive work of Jesus Christ, Christians expect the final healing, liberation and restoration of the whole of creation from the destructive powers of darkness and evil and look forward to the day when Christ is to recapitulate and consummate the whole creation in the eternal kingdom of God (cf. Rom. 8:22f., and paras 268-271).

83. Thus the creation is not only preserved by God, but he is also its supreme Lord, *governing* everything in creation according to his will and leading it according to his plans towards the final consummation, not letting it to the destructive consequences of the powers of evil. God is at work in all things to bring good out of evil (Gen. 50:20). Thus the visible and invisible creation reflects and testifies to the glory of the Triune God who creates, sustains, and governs it in anticipation of the coming kingdom, though human beings may not be able to recognize that by themselves.

The responsibility of humanity in creation

84. In the Christian perspective humankind has been created in the image and likeness of its Creator (Gen. 1:26-27). As such, humankind is given a permanent dignity which requires respect for human life (Gen. 9.6). It entails praise of the creation and the Creator. At the same time human beings are given *responsibility* to be God's representatives. They are co-operators in, stewards of, and even rulers over, creation (Gen. 1:26ff.; Ps. 8:4-8) — to care for all that is created, human beings, animals and plants and all the resources of the earth. This implies that human beings are free to develop a world of culture, including, among other things, the arts as well as science and technology, and to celebrate and use them under God.

85. In recent times the charge has been made that the biblical command to be stewards of, and even rulers over, creation has contributed to developments which threaten to destroy creation. But this distortion of stewardship developed where the commission to rule over the world has been divorced, in a process of emancipation, from accountability to the Creator. It also occurred where Christians misunderstood the biblical command in terms of unlimited human autonomy leading to abusive domination over creation and a neglect of the proper

stewardship owed to the Triune God. Understood in its true context and meaning, however, the biblical command calls human beings to become co-operators with God's work to preserve and consummate his creation.

The threat of destruction and God's act to save his creation

86. It is the reality of human sin which distorts human stewardship and threatens creation. Humanity refuses to be accountable to God, arrogates to itself the lordship over creation and thus places itself in the position of God. As a consequence creation is abused and human life is destroyed. In disobeying God's commandment, humanity abuses God's good creation for selfish purposes through the exploitation of nature and the destruction of the environment and of human beings, and through the use of science and technology for destroying life instead of furthering it.

87. In Jesus Christ God has acted to save his creation. Through Jesus Christ, the firstborn of new creation, God has renewed and continues to renew humanity. Women and men are continuously set free to rediscover and renew their stewardship in relation to God's creation.

Ethics of creation

88. This restoration of human beings in Christ establishes for Christians an ethical responsibility in dealing with creation and the environment. Such an ethic demands that women and men surrender the inordinate advantages which they arrogated to themselves in the process of gaining control over nature. The Christian faith in creation calls for a more careful and responsible use of science and technology, for resistance against the destruction of human beings and to affirm a preference for human life and relationships over material things.

89. Creation itself is alive because of the dynamic power of the Spirit of God working in it. To delight in creation, to join in its praise of God, is not merely legitimate: it is also right. This delight enables human beings to face their task. Not to be involved in this task is to join the destructive powers of evil at work in creation. But even where these powers are at work, Christians are assured in hope that the destiny of creation will remain in God's hands. God will bring the creation to its fulfilment in a new heaven and a new earth. Therefore, Christians can even now give honour, praise and glory to God the Father of all good things, who sent his Son to redeem his creation and who through his Holy Spirit gives new life to it until he will bring it to its final fulfilment.

PART II

We Believe in
One Lord Jesus Christ

A. JESUS CHRIST — INCARNATE FOR OUR SALVATION

90. The Church confesses, worships and serves Jesus Christ as Lord. This confession rests upon a single central acknowledgement that in Jesus we encounter God as our Saviour. In acknowledging this, the Creed makes three *affirmations*.
a) In Christ God directly manifests himself to us and enters into a new relationship with us.
b) Jesus is not only the eternal Son of the Father, he is also fully human and in him human nature is entirely restored and transformed by God's gracious presence.
c) Through Christ's incarnation "for us and for our salvation" God is present and living in the midst of human circumstances — even in poverty, pain and death — which are rarely annoointed with God

91. These affirmations are exposed to a number of *challenges*:
a) The idea of a pre-existent being who becomes incarnate in Jesus Christ and that this can result in a genuine human life seems strange to the modern mind. It is considered to be mythological. Furthermore, the assertions about the relationship of the pre-existent Son to the Father are suspected of owing more to ancient Greek metaphysics than to the biblical witness of Jesus Christ. Accordingly, the confession of Jesus Christ as the Son of God incarnate is often replaced by modern views of Jesus as a hero, a mystic, a religious teacher and genius, a revolutionary or a moral example.
b) The Christian doctrine that God's only Son became incarnate in Jesus of Nazareth is seen as constituting a major point of inter-religious controversy because it leads to affirming the unique and absolute importance of Jesus Christ for all human beings.

c) The Christian belief in the incarnation of God's son for our salvation
    appears as contradicted by continuing experiences of evil, suffering
    and death in personal as well as social life, because of which God
    does seem no less remote from our world than he was before the birth
    and ministry of Jesus Christ.

I. The Creed and its biblical witness

a) The text of the Creed

> 92. "We believe in one Lord, Jesus Christ,
>   the only Son of God,
>   eternally begotten of the Father,
>   Light from Light,
>   true God from true God, begotten, not made,
>   of one Being with the Father;
>   through him all things were made.
>   For us humans and for our salvation,   All
>   he came down from heaven:
>   was incarnate of
>   the Holy Spirit and the Virgin Mary,
>   and was made human."

> (AC: "I believe in Jesus Christ,
> God's only Son, our Lord,
> who was conceived by the Holy Spirit,
> born of the Virgin Mary.")

93. The Creed stresses that there "was no time" when God existed as a
solitary and undifferentiated being, as a potential Father without a Son.
The Son is eternal, springing from the Father as light streams from a
flame without interval or interruption. What the Father is and does, the
Son is and does also. The Father is Creator, but not alone; as Father of the
Son, he creates with and through the Son.

94. The most difficult and controversial expression in this section of
the Creed is the *homoousios* — "of one being with the Father". The main
point behind the use of this word was to exclude any idea that the Son was
a different kind of reality from the Father, contingent and created. On the
contrary, the Son, though dependent on the Father, is inseparable from
the life of the Father: the Son lives, as the Father lives, in unconditional
love, freedom, eternity, creativity. Thus God exists always in relation, as
a movement of love poured out and returned, of giving and responding.

As later Church Fathers (e.g. Gregory of Nazianzus) were to put it, the word "God" means nothing other than the life which is actively shared by Father, Son and Spirit. The specific significance of the intention expressed by the *homoousios* lies in the fact that our salvation in Christ was brought about by none other than God.

95. Although the Nicene-Constantinopolitan Creed makes no statement about the *mode* of the unity existing between Jesus and the eternal Son, the Council of Chalcedon in the fifth century explained and defined it by the concept of "hypostatic union" of the two natures in Christ: the divine and the human nature are not confused with one another or divided from one another, but the human nature is given its particular and unique mode of being because it is entirely sustained by the active presence of the eternal Word. Thus the divine Word does not replace any part of the human existence of Jesus, but acts through his complete humanity.

Commentary
 The detailed formulations about Christ as incarnate Son of God have to be understood in the *context* of the Christological debates of the early fourth century. The crisis of this period was not, strictly speaking, about "the incarnation": all parties agreed that Jesus was not wholly to be described or understood as a human being. What was at issue was the nature of what became incarnate.

 In the debate leading to the Council of Nicea (325), *Arius* claimed that God the Father alone is without cause, hence he is the only true God, while everything else including the Son was caused by him to exist. Only the Father needs nothing other than himself, and has no natural relation to anything beyond himself. He may choose to become a "Father" by bringing into being a creature whom he chooses to treat as a son; but this relationship is not part of what it is to be God. It depends only on his will. The Son need not exist, and has no natural kinship with God in himself. This teaching of Arius was rejected by the Church at the Council of Nicea (325).

b) Biblical witness
 96. The Creed assumes the pre-existence and divinity of Jesus Christ who is confessed as "true God from true God", "eternally begotten of the Father" and "through whom all things were made". Although the actual term *homoousios* does not occur in biblical language, the Creed is

throughout materially "biblical", and it is evident that the fathers of Nicea and Constantinople found support for Christ's divinity in the New Testament itself.

97. The most clear-cut references are found in the *Johannine writings*. In the Gospel of John, Jesus is presented as the Logos become flesh at a certain point in time (John 1:14), his glory being none other than the glory of God himself (v. 15). In other words, the Logos is pre-existent and divine. Indeed, before his incarnation, he "was God" (v. 1), "all things were made through him, and without him was not anything made that was made" (v. 2). Before his death, Jesus prays to the Father: "And now, Father, glorify thou me in thy own presence with the glory which I had with thee before the world was made" (17:5; see v. 24); "the glory which thou hast given me I have given to them, that they may be one even as we are one" (v. 22). After the resurrection, Thomas confesses Jesus as "Lord and God" (20:28).

98. In the Book of Revelation, in the same breath in which God is addressed *as God*, Jesus Christ, the "Lamb", is addressed in glorification and prayers (5:13; 7:10). Indeed, they are both the temple of the new Jerusalem (21:22); both are seated on the same divine throne (22:1, 3). This is why Jesus Christ is presented as God himself: the "one who is coming soon" (22:7,12,20); the one who "sent [his] angel to [John] with the testimony to the churches" (v. 16); as well as the one who is "the Alpha and the Omega, the first and the last, the beginning and the end" (v. 13; see also 1:8), like God himself (21:6).

99. There are a number of other biblical passages that were taken by the Church Fathers as witnessing to the unity of Jesus Christ as Son with the eternal God, while modern exegetical scholarship considers them as more ambiguous. This especially applies to the idea of pre-existence: it is not completely clear that the pre-existent Son is divine on the same level of divinity as the Father is.

100. In *Hebrews*, the Son is pre-existent (1:2) and reflects the glory of God and "bears the very stamp of his nature" (v. 3). Ps. 102:25-27 which speaks of God as the Creator (1:10-12) is quoted as being expressly addressed to the Son (1:8). Moreover, in the same verse the Son is addressed "O God" in the words of Ps. 45:6.

101. The *Pauline Epistles*. In Colossians there is a hymn in which Christ is spoken of as pre-existent and divine: "image of the invisible God... in him all things were created, in heaven and on earth, visible and invisible... He is before all things... For in Him all the fullness of God was pleased to dwell" (1:15-17, 19). The last assertion is taken up later:

"For in him the whole fullness of deity dwells bodily" (2:9), which is close to the Johannine statement in John 1:14.

102. In Philippians we find another hymn that speaks of Christ's divinity as well as incarnation: "... though he was in the form of God, did not count equality with God a thing to hold on, but emptied himself, taking the form of a servant, being born in the likeness of men. And being found in human form ..." (2:6-8). Whether this hymn is — fully or partly — pre-Pauline or not, it is evident that it reflects Paul's thought. Thus, Pauline texts that speak of the Son's sending (Rom. 8:3; Gal. 4:4) could be taken as referring to the incarnation of the pre-existent Son, disregarding the question whether such statements originally were meant to speak merely of Christ's mission.

103. In any case, the content of 1 Corinthians 8:6, whether Pauline or pre-Pauline, reflects Paul's view that Christ's "Lordship" is fully comparable with God's [the Father's] "divinity". This is evident from vv. 4-5 where the *one* God is opposed to the idols which are referred to as the *many* "gods" and "lords".

104. Last but not least, one should consider Paul's praying to Christ in 2 Cor. 12:8 and also 1 Thess. 3:11-12. In the latter instance, God the Father and the Lord Jesus are invoked as one (v. 11). The starting point for such an attitude may well have been the *Maranatha* (Come, Lord [Jesus]) of the very early Christian tradition (1 Cor. 16:22; Rev. 22:20; see also v. 17). In this case, and considering the structure and formulation of Rom. 9:5b, Christ may well have been addressed as "God" in Paul's "blessing" there; see the similar "glorification" addressed to Christ in Heb. 13:21.

105. In his earthly ministry, Jesus claimed a unique relationship with the God of Israel to whom he turned in prayer, addressing him intimately as "Abba" (Luke 11:2; Mark 14:36). He was recognized as teaching with unique authority that left people amazed (Mark 1:25). The same authority was perceived by those who witnessed his deeds of healing (Mark 2:12). His unique relationship with the Father came to expression in the title Son of God, which was given to him on the occasion of his baptism (Mark 1:11 par.) and of his transfiguration (Mark 9:7). In the infancy narrative of Luke, Jesus is accorded this title even from his conception (Luke 1:32, 35).

106. Contemporary biblical studies by and large follow the historico-critical methodology. Their approach to the study of the person of Jesus Christ starts with Jesus of Nazareth in his historical setting, and their study of early Church Christology is seen against the background of the

different world-views existent in the first century AD Eastern Mediterranean, especially in Palestinian and Hellenistic Judaism. Consequently, Jesus' "divinity" and "pre-existence" are considered as expressions of the significance of the human person Jesus of Nazareth. His earthly ministry and his resurrection, as witnessed by the apostles, form the point of departure for any contemporary study of Christology. That seems to create a tension between this approach and the "Nicene" approach.

107. However, it has to be realized that the "Nicene" approach is doxological and confessional. It does not seek to retrace the steps by which the early Christians came to develop their Christological confession or rehearse the arguments that may have helped them on their way. This approach occurs as early as New Testament hymns such as Phil. 2:6-11 and Col. 1:15-20. It is also found in Rom. 1:3-4, 8:3 and Gal. 4:4.

108. One might argue that the entire patristic approach from early times followed the "confessional" line. They accepted the story of Jesus, as witnessed to in the Gospels and in all parts of the New Testament, while they read it particularly from the perspective of the Gospel of John. This allowed them to establish the crucial link between Jesus and the Creator of the world, whose eternal Word became manifest in the life of Jesus. The same concern is evident in the formulation of the Nicene Creed where Jesus is referred to as "true God from true God" (cf. John 1:1). This language strongly suggests the Johannine prologue as background.

109. The modern approach of historical exegesis need not exclude the patristic "confessional" approach nor does the latter exclude the analysis of the growth of the Christological tradition. The two approaches are compatible and may even enrich each other, as long as the possibility is not dismissed — that from the earliest stages of the tradition there has been present implicitly that which only later became explicitly stated. This means that the eternal Son and Word of God was one with the human reality of Jesus from its beginning, although the explicit formulation of this fact developed in the course of the Christological tradition.

II. Explication for today

One Lord Jesus Christ

110. The Christian confession recognizing Jesus Christ as one Lord is rooted in his resurrection from the dead by God's own power. The resurrection confirms the life and deeds of Jesus as the eternal word of God spoken for us and our salvation. The ambiguity surrounding his teaching and behaviour, and his claim to possess an authority beyond all

human authority which led to his crucifixion, was removed by the Easter event. As a result of this divine confirmation in the resurrection the Creed ascribes universal and eternal divine authority to Jesus, who is to be recognized and obeyed as the Lord over all and everything else (Phil. 2:9-11). There are no human beings, no realms or levels which are not under the promise and the commandment of the *one* Lord Jesus Christ. There are many authorities and powers in the world, but Christians confess Jesus Christ as the one and only Lord in the same way as they believe in one God, the Father of the universe (cf. 1 Cor. 8:5f.).

The Only Son of God
111. To the modern mind, it is not easy to grasp what the Scriptures and the Creed referred to when they spoke of the Son of God. To many it seems self-evident that if there is a God at all, his reality is absolutely unique and transcendent so that there can be nothing to associate with him. This, however, is also true of the God of the Jewish faith whom Jesus addressed as Father. Since the one God is indeed utterly transcendent, defying every human attempt at naming and categorizing, it is quite extraordinary that Jesus related to this transcendent God with such familiarity as to call him Father. He claimed to be the only one who had a right to do so, and this prerogative was expressed by referring to himself as the Son: "no one knows the Father except the Son and any one to whom the Son chooses to reveal him" (Matt. 11:27). God's identity as Father — in the sense that word assumed in Christian usage — is brought into view only in the way in which Jesus revealed God as the Father by showing himself to be his absolutely devoted Son.

112. The word "Son" does not only refer to the human person of Jesus in his unique relationship to his heavenly Father, but already in Paul's letters it refers to a pre-existent being who was sent in the flesh by the Father (Rom. 8:3; Gal. 4:4f.; cf. Phil. 2:6). In a modern perspective, this appears to many as a mythological conception. But to be related to the Son belongs to the eternal being of God the Father. Thus the Son, who became manifest in Jesus' relationship with the Father, is himself eternal and therefore precedes the historical birth and ministry of Jesus. Therefore, the conception of a pre-existent Son who became incarnate in Jesus Christ must not be dismissed. Though the language of the Creed may appear strange in beginning its assertions about Jesus Christ with this idea of pre-existent sonship, it thereby makes a substantial point: the human reality of Jesus in relation to God the Father can only be understood as manifestation of the eternal God. To be eternal does not only apply to the

one to whom Jesus related, but also to the Son who in such a way relates to the Father.

113. The confession of the eternal sonship of Jesus of Nazareth is also of soteriological significance for all times. The love which Jesus embodied, the authority with which he announced the nearness of the kingdom of God and the forgiveness of sins, his solidarity with the poor and outcast and finally his suffering and death — all this would have been an episode in history had not people experienced in these signs and events the love, presence and even the suffering of God himself. Because the Son of God was with God from eternity, it was God who came in his Son into their midst and continues, through the power of the Holy Spirit, to be present and active among us. Thus our trust in life and death is not in a human being blessed and used by God, but in the Son of God from eternity to eternity.

114. In the Scriptures, Jesus is not the only one to be called "son" of God. The word was used before of the Davidic king in his capacity to represent the rule of God on earth (2 Sam. 7:14; Ps. 2:7). It was extended to the people of Israel in view of their special relationship to the God of the covenant (e.g. Hos. 11:1; Jer. 31:9). But Jesus is in a unique way the Son of God because it is only in relation to him that God is definitively revealed as Father. The use of the word "son" in the Old Testament, then, foreshadows the sonship of Jesus, but it is he who is the only Son of the Father because the eternal Son and his relationship to the Father became incarnate in him. When Paul applies the word "sons" to Christians (Rom. 8:16; Gal. 4:5f.), it is because of our participation through faith and baptism in Jesus Christ, the only Son of God, and in his relationship to the Father.

Eternally begotten of the Father

115. The Creed emphasizes that the origin of the Son from the Father is in eternity and not in time. Otherwise, the eternal God would not be fully present in the Son, and Jesus as incarnate Son of God, born in time, could not communicate to the faithful a communion with the eternal God himself. That the Son was "begotten" of the Father is an image taken from Luke 3:22 and Heb. 1:5, where Ps. 2:7 is quoted, but the same idea was also often found in the term "only begotten", which especially occurs in the Gospel of John (e.g. 1:14, 18 and 3:16, 18), but actually means no more than the "only" one. The word "begotten" expressed the connatural relationship between Father and Son, and since the Father is eternal, the begetting of the Son did not occur at some particular time, but is itself

eternal. The Creed explicates this connatural character of the relationship between Father and Son in the assertions that follow:

Light from light, true God from true God, begotten, not made, of one being with the Father

116. The Son belongs to God as light comes from the source of light. It is of the same nature as its source is, and so the Son is of the same nature as the Father is: true God from true God. He is no creature, but belongs in eternity to the Father, because in all eternity God is not conceivable as Father without the Son in whom his fatherhood is expressed. Here, the word "begotten" is used again, because it lends itself to distinguish the Son's relationship to the Father from the creatures that are "made" by God. Creatures need not exist, and creatures did not always exist. But God the Father was never without his Son.

117. In eternity God the Father is not alone, but exists as a person in relationship. And yet there is no more than one God, nor is anything other than God associated with him, for Father and Son are of one being. In the incarnate Son there is no other God than the one God. The famous and once (in the fourth century) controversial phrase "of one being with the Father" *(homoousios)* makes sure that the Christian confession of the divine sonship of Jesus Christ does not surrender the monotheistic character of the biblical faith in God.

118. Because of its several biblical references Christians associate the phrase "light from light" in the Creed also with their experience that they have found in Jesus an illumination and orientation for their lives in the "darkness" of the world. In Jesus, who is the light of the world (John 8:12), the Creator and Redeemer is present and active, who separates the light from the darkness, saying "let there be light" (Gen. 1:3). The light which is in Jesus Christ and is given through the Holy Spirit to us is totally different from all other illuminations and orientations offered by self-appointed gurus and saviours today.

Through him all things were made

119. According to the New Testament, all things have been created through the Son (Col. 1:16; Heb. 1:2). This is consistent with the Christian faith in the one God who created the world, because the Son is believed to be one with the Father. Thus he is also involved in the creation of the world. The early Christians recognized him in the "word" of the Creator, which in the biblical story (Gen. 1:3ff.) was mentioned as his means in creating the world (cf. John 1:3). The word of creation also

includes the design of its order (cf. Prov. 8:22ff.), which our human conceptions of natural law can only perceive in approximate ways. All of creation was designed from the beginning to be brought to completion in the Son (Eph. 1:10). In creating the world, the creative love of the Father already looked towards the incarnation of the eternal Son at the culmination of history. He is the eternal model, the "Logos" of all creation, epitomizing what each creature in its particular way is to be. No creature can attain fulfilment without him. In the light of this assertion the significance of the incarnation of the Son becomes fully apparent.

For us humans and for our salvation he... was incarnate

120. That the eternal Son became incarnate in Jesus of Nazareth is an affirmation summarizing the entire course of Jesus' earthly ministry as seen from the perspective of his resurrection. The incarnation, thus, is not only related to the beginning of Jesus' human life. It is related to his ministry and mission for the *salvation* of the people of Israel, of all humanity and creation. Amongst the various understandings of ways of salvation are the following:

a) In the mission of the Son the eternal love of the Father for all of his creatures becomes manifest in his self-giving to the point of death.

b) The power of death which is the consequence of our turning away from God is overcome. Communion with the Father is restored through the Son in the power of the Spirit.

c) The Father in his unconditional and infinite mercy accepts the sinner who turns to him thus restoring the communion with him that was lost through sin. This happens when we share in the sonship of Jesus himself and in his relation to his Father, when in his Spirit we are liberated to address the Father as "Abba" in our prayers, and to entrust ourselves to his loving concern.

d) The consequence of salvation is that we are called to be faithful and obedient sons and daughters of God authoritatively proclaiming God's acceptance, living already in the kingdom as far as we are able, living out the values of the kingdom, welcoming the outcast, oppressed and helpless, identifying with the suffering and confronting the risk implicit in the attempt to live in this way in a world which still resists the love of God and its demands.

Of the Holy Spirit and the Virgin Mary

121. On the basis of the New Testament witness, the Creed confirms that the incarnation of the Son of God took place by the power of the *Holy*

Spirit. The Scripture commonly associates the Holy Spirit with the work of creation and new creation. The eschatological completion of humankind and of all creation, inaugurated in the resurrection of Jesus Christ, the new Adam, is penetrated by the pressure of the life-giving Spirit. And so when Christ came to redeem and renew humankind, his very conception was the work of the same Spirit that animated humankind at its first creation. The Holy Spirit who overshadowed Mary (Luke 1:35) is the Holy Spirit by whose power Jesus was raised from the dead (Rom. 8:11). The same Spirit is now given to those who by faith and through baptism into Christ are born "not of blood nor of the will of the flesh nor of the will of men, but of God" (John 1:13). It is given them as a pledge of their future share in the new and everlasting life of the resurrection. Moreover, it is the same Spirit who will bring about the transfiguration of all creation to share in the glory of God. When the Creed attributes to the power of the Holy Spirit the incarnation of the One through whom all things are made, it relates this event to the whole world, its renewal and its consummation.

122. All Christians share in the confession affirmed by the Council of Ephesus (431) that *Mary* is "Theotokos", the mother of him who is also God, through the creative work of the Spirit of God. In referring to the motherhood of Mary, the Creed shows the Son of God to be a human being like us, one who shares our experience in being born and loved by a mother, and nurtured by parental care. But Mary is also the disciple who hears the word of God, responds to it and keeps it. In her obedience to God and her utter dependence on the Holy Spirit, Mary is the example par excellence of our discipleship. Since the first centuries, she has been seen as representing the daughter of Sion, waiting for the accomplishment of the messianic promises and of the coming kingdom.

123. In her complete reliance on God, her active response of faith and her expectation of the kingdom, Mary has been seen as a figure *(typos)* of and an example for the Church. Like Mary, the Church cannot exist on its own; it can only rely on God; it is the vigilant servant waiting for the return of the Master.

124. In affirming the *virginity* of Mary, the Creed expresses the belief that the Father of her son at his temporal birth is the same as the one whose Son he is from all eternity, "eternally begotten of the Father".

Commentary

Some Christians today feel difficulties with the affirmation of Mary's virginity. For some, this is because they consider that such a miraculous birth would be inconsistent with God's way of acting towards his people. Others do not reject in principle the possibility of God's miraculous action. But they do not find in the New Testament any evidence other than the infancy narratives whose literary form does not necessarily imply a historical claim concerning Mary's virginity. The point of the narratives, they say, is to affirm the divine origin and sonship of Jesus Christ, without specifying the manner in which the incarnation has been realized.

When the Creed *brings together* the phrases "by the Holy Spirit" and "from the Virgin Mary", it is confessing that Jesus Christ is both God and man.

And was made human

125. In the way that he is human, in his words and deeds, his anger and love, Jesus embodied fully true humanity. Jesus shows us humanity as it should be and can become, in him, by the power of God's presence in our midst. The belief that Jesus became man for us enables us not to despair of ourselves or of history nor to consider it meaningless. Christ is even now woven into the fabric of the human story, transfiguring the past, present and future. Through him, we are to acknowledge our historical dependence, our need for others, and the claim of others' needs upon us. We cannot exist as abstract, autonomous individuals without a past or a context; our freedom is a freedom not to run from our limitations but to respond to them with creative and transforming action.

126. Like each one of us Jesus is a human individual. This entails specificity of time, space, gender, race, social-cultural context, etc. This reality of Jesus' specificity, willed by God, encourages each one of us to accept his or her own specificities, who we are and where we are, not passively but in an imaginative, critical, exploring way. Jesus' life is capable of showing unconditional trust in God and love for God's world; any limited life, however frustrated or apparently diminished, can therefore be transfigured to show forth the truth and love of God. In God's eyes, every human life has the chance of reflecting the life of Christ.

B. JESUS CHRIST — SUFFERING AND CRUCIFIED FOR OUR SAKE

127. From the time of the earliest New Testament witness and throughout the centuries, the Church has confessed that Jesus Christ

suffered and was crucified for us. The theological significance and focus of this confession is indicated by *for our sake*. These words point to the decisive saving event, which comprehends in its scope all human beings. Such confession is made on the basis and in the perspective of Christ's resurrection.

128. The confession that Jesus Christ suffered and was crucified *for our sake* is made today in a world which is marked by the struggle between the forces of life and the forces of sin, suffering and death. Therefore, the *challenges* — posed by Christians and non-Christians alike — to the faith we express in this affirmation of the Creed are: How can the universal condition of sin with all its consequences be changed by the suffering and crucifixion of the one person of Jesus Christ? Is it appropriate to speak of an involvement of the Jewish people in the suffering and death of Jesus? What is the relevance of the confession of the suffering and crucifixion of Christ for us in the face of the human condition of suffering and death and for the struggles of Christians and others against these realities?

I. The Creed and its biblical witness

a) The text of the Creed

129. "For our sake he was crucified under Pontius Pilate;
he suffered and was buried."

(AC; "He suffered under Pontius Pilate,
was crucified, died and was buried.
He descended to the dead.")

130. In the Nicene-Constantinopolitan Creed the crucifixion, suffering and burial of Christ are the only data concerning his human life beside the fact of his birth. The death of Christ is given in the Creed a comparatively brief reference when compared with the preceding section which deals with the divine nature and incarnation of Christ. This brevity is readily understood when the context of the Arian controversy is taken into account; but it has a positive import as well, for it makes absolutely clear that the one who was crucified, suffered and was buried was none other than the eternal Son of God who became a human being.

131. The phrase "under Pontius Pilate" indicates that the death and suffering of Jesus Christ is a specific historical event in world history. "And was buried" underlines the fact that Jesus died a real death on the cross and was resurrected from that death.

132. The phrase "for our sake" also appears in the preceding formulation concerning the incarnation and expresses thereby the link between the incarnation and the death of Jesus and their saving character for humanity.

b) Biblical witness

133. Concerning the death and resurrection of Jesus Christ the Nicene Creed follows one of the oldest credal formulae found in the New Testament: "Christ died for our sins ... was buried, was raised on the third day in accordance with the scriptures" (1 Cor. 15:3-4). The notion of Christ's death for our sake, i.e. for our sins, occurs in the Pauline epistles (Rom. 3:25; 5:8; 6:6-7; 8:32; 2 Cor. 5:15, 18-21; Gal. 1:4; 2:20; 3:13; Eph. 2:13,16) as well as in the rest of the New Testament (Matt. 20:28/10:45; Acts 3:18f.; 1 Pet. 1:18-19; Heb. 9:15; Rev. 1:5; 5:9; 7:14; 12:10f.; 14:4); besides, it is at the heart of the most ancient tradition of the eucharistic words. This understanding of Christ's death as vicarious explains the importance given to Isa. 53 in the New Testament and early Christian literature.

134. The notion of vicariousness is intimately linked with that of sacrifice, as is evident from the same Isa. 53. Christ's death as sacrifice is attested already in Paul (Rom. 3:24f.; 1 Cor. 5:7; and 2 Cor. 25:21, if one takes *hamartia* here to mean the Old Testament sacrifice *hatta't*). In 1 Pet. 1:18f. Christ is likened to a sacrificial lamb. This notion becomes central in the Johannine writings (John 1:29; Rev. 5:6). On the other hand, the aspect of voluntariness in Christ's sacrifice (Gal. 1:4; 2:20; Phil. 2:7) may have been behind the view of Jesus Christ as high priest (John 17; Heb. 6-10).

135. However, one cannot but notice the precedence given to the crucifixion in the Nicene Creed. One need only compare the "he suffered under Pontius Pilate, was crucified, died and was buried" of the Apostles' Creed, to the "for our sake he was crucified under Pontius Pilate; he suffered and was buried" of the Nicene Creed. In the latter, the death is not mentioned, and the suffering is referred to *after* the crucifixion. The practical equation in Christian traditional terminology of Christ's crucifixion and his death is chiefly due to Paul.

136. In the *Pauline epistles*, Christ's crucifixion is another way to speak of his atoning death (Eph. 2:16; Col. 1:20; 2:13f.); dying with Christ is expressed through being crucified with him (Rom. 6:6; Gal. 2:20). Even more: the "cross of Christ" is another name for Paul's gospel itself (1 Cor. 1:13,17-18,23; 2:2; Gal. 3:1; 6:12; Phil. 3:18). Conse-

quently, the "cross" is another expression for the new reality (Gal. 6:14; also 5:24) which is otherwise called the *kaine ktisis* (2 Cor. 5:17).

137. The reason for that is not the horrible suffering bound to the crucifixion, but rather the "shamefulness" connected therewith in the Roman world. Indeed, the *skandalon* of Paul's gospel *is* the cross (Gal. 5:11; 1 Cor. 1:23; see also Phil. 2:8). Paul does not even shy from quoting scripture itself to say that Christ became a "curse" (!) in his death by crucifixion (Gal. 3:13); yet, it is this death on the cross that secured us the blessing of Abraham (v. 14) which is nothing else than the gospel itself (v. 8).

138. This notion of shame seems to be present in the *synoptic tradition*, found in Mark 8:31-9:1/Luke 9:22-27, which deals with Jesus' first introduction of his apostles to the idea of his death. His foretelling of his death is followed by the invitation that his followers carry their cross as well as the warning that "whoever is ashamed of me ... of him will also be ashamed the Son of Man ..." The same connection — and in this case, quite unexpected — between cross and shame occurs in Heb. 12:2 in a context where the Christians are asked to follow the example of Jesus (vv. 1-3).

139. In *John*, the meaning of Jesus' crucifixion is taken one step further. It is not only the way towards his glorification (Phil. 2:8-11), rather his ascending on the cross is actually equated with his ascending into glory (3:13-15; 8:21-30; 12:27-34). This is in tune with the Johannine Logos theology: Jesus himself is "the resurrection and the life" (11:25; see 1:4)

140. Jesus' suffering was central to the earliest Christologies. This can be seen in the detailed traditions concerning his last days in Jerusalem. The suffering of the Messiah was scandalous (see Judas' reaction) since the Messiah, by definition, is the overcoming and victorious one. This explains why the "Holy Week" tradition in the earliest gospel, Mark, is presented against the background of Ps. 22. The choice was perfect since such an approach (a) gives weight to Jesus' sufferings (Ps. 22:12-18); (b) indicates that they are ultimately for the sake of others (vv. 22-28); (c) foresees the ultimate victory after the forsakenness (vv. 24, 31); (d) allows the reading that the sufferings were willed by God and were an integral part of God's economy (vv. 1-8; 27-31).

141. The mention of Jesus' burial was part of the earliest confessions (1 Cor. 15:4) and was rendered in detail in the Gospels (Matt. 27:57-61; Mark 15:42-47; Luke 23:50-55; John 19:38-42). The reason is at least twofold: (a) Jesus *did* die; his death was not only apparent; (b) his

resurrection was a *divine* action (Acts 2:32; Rom. 1:4). Both aspects are entwined in the very old and central tradition of the "empty tomb".

II. Explication for today

He was crucified for us

142. Christians believe that human beings — individually and collectively — live in bondage to sin and death. Sin separates them from God and from one another by their turning away from the source of life which is God the Creator. They seek to justify themselves by their own efforts and achievements and live a life without reference to God. The consequence of this universal condition of sin is the universal dominion of death (cf. Rom. 5:12ff.). The New Testament understanding of death is not restricted to the event of individual death. It also comprises everything that surrounds death like the powers of evil, decay and corruption in individual and social life. This perception of the human condition is reflected in general human experience, where human self-centredness, egoism and striving for power over others manifests itself in the attitudes of groups of people and in many contemporary social, political and economic structures: unjust and oppressive forms and conditions of life, hunger, imposed poverty, exploitation, discrimination, anxiety in the face of armed conflicts, and in many other ways. These consequences of sin cause hatred, suffering, despair and death among human beings, and lead humankind to disrupt the natural order and to threaten the very existence of our world.

The situation created by sin and its consequence, death, is also a manifestation of God's judgment, in that, as the apostle says, "he gives humanity up to uncleanness through the lusts of their own hearts" (Rom. 1:24, cf. 26 and 28).

143. In which way is the gospel of the suffering and death of Christ the *Good News* for all people? In the light of his resurrection we see in Christ's suffering and death God's action, the fulfilment of God's saving purpose for all people, by which he destroyed the power of death. He took away the guilt from humanity and he created the prototype of new life for those who follow Jesus. This is the Good News which is paradoxically bound up with the scandalous character of Jesus' cross which judges the securities and claims of the world. Therefore, the Church must never cease to preach Christ crucified (1 Cor. 1:18-25; 2:2; Gal 5:11). It encourages Christians in their life and mission to follow the example of Christ and move "outside the city gates" (Heb. 13:12,13).

Commentary

The death of Christ has been understood (in the history of the Christian faith) in different ways. One type of interpretation is frequently found in the theology of the ancient church and is continued in the tradition of the Eastern Church in particular. Here, the death of Jesus Christ — God and human being — is seen as destroying *death's* power and influence, by which human beings are burdened and oppressed. The death and resurrection of Jesus is a victory by which human beings are liberated from death and all the powers of darkness.

Another type of interpretation is represented in the medieval and post-medieval West. Here the death of Jesus is understood as an atoning event in terms of an offering of satisfaction, whereby the *guilt* incurred by human beings in violating God's honour by their sin is removed.

There is a third type of interpretation found especially in modern theology. Here the dying of Jesus is seen in the perspective of his total faith and obedience. He remained *faithful* to his mission right to the very end. Thereby he became for us the prototype of a life which refuses to be diverted from its devotion to God and to other human beings and which witnesses to God as the loving and merciful one through the quality, depth and cost of its trust.

On the basis of the biblical witness as outlined above, the real concerns implicit in these interpretations are not alternatives. They emphasize particular aspects of that witness and should be held together.

144. In his suffering and dying *for us*, Jesus, 'despite all the hostility and pain inflicted upon him by the people and the authorities, did not abandon his mission of love, but persisted in it — that very same love in whose strength he displayed to his fellow human beings the unconditional love of the Father. Jesus' death is not a condition in the sense that the Father's love requires such an expiatory offering; rather it was from the beginning the universal saving initiative and purpose of God to send his son into the world and even let him die for the reconciliation of the world. Jesus' life was thus lived within the human predicament which made his death on the cross inescapable: it was inevitable, in bringing the Father's boundless love into this world, that in his faithfulness to his divine mission to proclaim and enact the kingdom of God (Luke 11:20, cf. 17:21), Jesus took the place of the sinner and had to suffer such demonstration of hostility which led to his death. Coming into a world that is under the judgement of God, Christ experienced in his suffering

and death the consequences of human sin. He was sent by God "in the likeness of sinful flesh and for sin" (Rom. 8:3), as one who was himself without sin, he was regarded as a sinner and became a victim of the curse of the law in order to liberate us from its curse (Gal. 3:13). As Lamb of God he carried the sins of the world (Isa. 53:4-7; John 1:29).

145. In this sense, Jesus' sacrifice of suffering and death, his self-offering in the place and for the sake of others has become the salvation of the world because this was the way in which God was reconciling the world to himself. The message of the *reconciliation* accomplished in the death of Jesus is for all people the offer of liberation, through justification and the forgiveness of sins received in faith, as well as the gift of new life in the Holy Spirit. God relieves consciences burdened by sin and guilt. Christians experience this acceptance in spite of their guilt and without the pressure of having to merit such acceptance by their own deeds. This is a comforting and liberating experience, but also an incentive to struggle against sin and not evade responsibility in personal and social life.

146. It is through faith and baptism that a human being dies with Christ and participates in the new life of his resurrection (cf. Rom. 6:3f.; Col. 3:3f.). This means to "walk in newness of life" (Rom. 6:4), being liberated from the vicious circle of self-justification and self-centredness, hatred and injury to neighbours, lack of gratitude towards God and disregard of God. Communion with Christ and his death strengthens people to overcome their fear and to live with confidence and readiness to forgive, thus challenging the deadly powers of hatred, alienation and mistrust by understanding, love and reconciliation. This is a process which also becomes effective in the social and political fields and in attitudes to the whole of creation as an impulse and call for renewal, respect and care.

147. The discipleship of a person so liberated by God's love is not however free from sin, suffering and death. But because our own death is already taken up into the death of Christ, in baptism, we are assured that even death cannot separate us from God's love in Christ Jesus (Rom. 8:38f.) and from all hope for future life. Thus, even in their weakness and vulnerability, Christians in their communion with Christ and through the power of the Holy Spirit are enabled to become co-workers of God. The way of powerlessness and humility is the way of divine wisdom (1 Cor. 1:18ff.); it is the way in which God's liberating and victorious action becomes effective in history.

Under Pontius Pilate

148. Particularly significant in this credal formulation is the phrase *under Pontius Pilate* which not only indicates that the death and suffering of the incarnate Son of God is a specific historical event, but today allows us to put it also in the wider context of world history and human political power. As the Creed's formulation "under" indicates, the execution of Jesus took place under the authority of the Roman governor Pontius Pilate. Pilate represents in general terms political oppression over an occupied country. He also represents, in the way he preserves his authority during the trial of Jesus, the violation of an individual's human rights for opportunistic reasons (cf. Mark 15:6-15). The statement that Jesus was crucified under Pontius Pilate indicates that his death was not a private but a public affair and that the end of his life was deeply interwoven with the political circumstances in Palestine at that time. This was a consequence of his and the disciples' witness to the kingdom. These implications were misused and misrepresented by his enemies. That Christ's life and death was in different ways intertwined with the social and political conditions of his native country is of significance for the life, commitment and death of his disciples today.

149. At certain times during the course of the centuries an attitude arose among Christians to accuse the past and present *Jewish people* of being guilty of the death of Jesus. Such attitudes continue today. Although there are passages in the passion story of the New Testament which refer to the Jewish people accepting the consequences of Jesus' death for themselves and their future generations, such as: "his blood be on us and on our children" (Matt. 27:25), a distinction must be made between the quoted Jewish voice from that time and God's own judgement over his chosen people. In any case such New Testament passages cannot be used to justify the long and painful history of anti-Jewish attitudes among Christians.

150. It was primarily certain small but influential circles of religious leaders, groups of Pharisees and Sadducees, who were involved in the events leading to Jesus' death. They opposed him because of his "blasphemous" claims, his criticism of religious authorities and his fundamentally different interpretation of the authority of the law. These religious leaders, as well as Pontius Pilate, exemplify the temptation for all authorities when confronted with the message of the kingdom of God.

151. As a *Jew*, Jesus was born, lived and died within the context of the Jewish people and their tradition. Thus the Messiah came from God's

chosen people. Because of this background of Jesus, any anti-Jewish interpretation of a number of biblical texts should be seen as a fundamental misunderstanding. The crucified One was of the chosen people of Israel and his death was for the Jewish people, though not for them only (John 11:51-53). His death did not put an end to Israel's election, but in the hands of God became a means to expand it into the election of Jews *and* Gentiles, of all humanity (cf. Eph. 2:14-18). For this the Father both of Jews and Gentiles is to be praised because through Christ's death he has broken down the enmity which stood like a dividing wall between Jews and Gentiles (Eph. 2:13-18). In creating the Church he has made the two into one undivided people, grafting the wild gentile olive shoot to the branches of the original olive tree (cf. Rom. 11:17).

He suffered

152. The announcement of the coming of the kingdom of God was the content of Jesus' preaching and actions, but also the ultimate cause of his suffering and death. His faithfulness to this divine mission was a manifestation of exemplary adherence to the will of the Father. For a humanity estranged from God this faithfulness was vicarious because Jesus submitted himself completely to the righteousness of God so that through his suffering and death all those who follow him are reconciled with God. Thus, the suffering and death of Christ is Good News for all people because it opens up, through the power of the Holy Spirit, new life and hope in the history of humanity.

153. The suffering and death of Christ is in a particular way good news for all people who suffer. In our world today many people *are* suffering. Although in Christ "the new has come" (2 Cor. 5:17), the whole creation, along with the children of God, continues to groan in the birth-pangs of the redemption of the children of God (Rom. 8:19-23). Individuals and groups of people alike *suffer* despair, from loneliness, illness and pain, physical and mental handicaps or natural calamities. Suffering may be self-inflicted, inflicted by others, or the result of tragic accidents. But there is also suffering which is freely accepted whenever people risk their lives in order to help and save others and to alleviate human suffering.

154. Despite all the identifiable causes and rational explanations of suffering and death a deeper question remains. Why is there *suffering and death at all?* Why does this kind of suffering happen to me and not to others? Why are my people trapped in the abyss of starvation while others are enjoying affluence and apparent security?

155. Behind these questions lies a protest against suffering and death as such. This protest finds explicit and constructive expression in the struggle of the forces of life against the forces of sin, suffering and death. Here is compassion with and sensitivity to the suffering. Many efforts are undertaken to improve the conditions of human life through medical care, social services and through changing those structures which inflict massive suffering and death. Religions, philosophies and ideologies seek in their way to sustain the struggle against suffering and death.

156. The question to the Creed is: What light is shed by our confession of the crucified Christ for us upon the human condition and the struggles it implies? The salvation offered through the suffering and death of Christ does not provide a simple explanation of or a cheap consolation for the reality of human suffering and death, but is God's response to it. In the suffering and cross of Jesus, God has taken upon himself in the person of his Son the condition of human death that is provoked by our sin and demonstrated his solidarity with human beings and his *compassion* for their suffering. God is on the side of human beings in the struggle with the powers of sin and death.

157. This has a twofold meaning for human existence under the power and fear of suffering and death. God is demonstrating to human beings that he is with them in these situations, that he is suffering where they are suffering — especially where there is no apparent reason in such suffering — and thereby gives them consolation and strength. God is also providing them with hope for a life that is no longer marked by death. Morever, God's solidarity enables them to *struggle* against suffering and death in all their manifestations. In the particular case of human oppression, the victim is assured that God is never on the side of the oppressor, the bringer of death, but will, in his justice, protect the rights and lives of the victims.

158. Because Christians are incorporated into Christ by baptism, they are led in many ways to suffer with him as they share in his obedience. The call to *discipleship* implies a readiness to take up one's own cross. Saying "yes" to God today runs the risk of entering into the destiny of Jesus Christ, of the "yes" to God for which he was crucified.

159. Christ uses this suffering for and with others to do his work of love and salvation through us. Such *suffering with Christ for others* has marked the life of many Christians, beginning with the first followers of Jesus and continuing through the centuries until today. This company of suffering witnesses includes the many well-known martyrs as well as millions of unknown Christians. Through their suffering participation in

Christ's sufferings they express in a realistic way the significance of the new life which overcomes all suffering, and they witness to this gift before their fellow human beings.

160. The suffering and the apparent scandal of the crucifixion of Jesus exposes the *unjust powers of this world.* The one who was innocent and just was crucified as a criminal; and this fact continues to uncover injustice that masquerades as justice. The crucifixion of Jesus exposes the cruelty of human beings and of the dominant religious and political powers. Although they appeared to triumph over God's righteous and loving Servant, their victory was shown to be a defeat by God's own victory in the resurrection. The apparent weakness of God proved to be stronger than the powers of this world. The justice of God condemns the injustice of all power that excludes and murders.

161. In the power of Christ's suffering, crucifixion and resurrection, all Christians and churches are called to continue to identify and confront inhuman and oppressive powers in this world. Looking back at those who claimed to serve God's will by crucifying his Son, Christians are enabled to identify the *idols* of status and security which seduce people from the worship and service of the true and only God. Such discernment must also include an awareness of the danger of a false triumphalism in the Church and among Christians, an attitude which obscures the true nature of God's victory in the cross and resurrection of his Son. Christians are called and empowered to be effective witnesses to Jesus Christ through their obedient suffering with him and in their resistance to and denunciation of all powers that seek to take the place of God.

C. JESUS CHRIST — RISEN
TO OVERCOME ALL EVIL POWERS

162. The Christ in whom Christians believe is the *living Christ* present among them in the living Word, in baptism, in the eucharist and in the sacramental and liturgical life of the Church. It is Jesus Christ present who allows Christians to accept and to offer forgiveness, to love and to bless each other and also to pray. Christians would have no hope in this world of death and hatred, were it not for the suffering Christ, the Risen One alive in their midst (cf. Gal. 2:20f.; Col. 3:1-14).

163. Such affirmations are faced with serious *challenges* today. How is it possible to believe in the resurrection of Jesus Christ in the midst of a

world where "resurrections do not take place"? How is belief in a resurrection of the dead and in the life of the age to come possible in a time marked by a certain kind of scientific-technological thinking? And how is belief in the life of the age to come to be understood in face of the limitations and possibilities present in a natural scientific world-view? How can the power of the Risen Christ become a source of strength, perseverance and hope over against the social, economic, ideological and other powers which seek to dominate our destiny?

I. The Creed and its biblical witness

a) The text of the Creed

    164. "On the third day he rose from the dead
        in accordance with the Scriptures;
        he ascended into heaven
        and is seated at the right hand of the Father.
        He will come again in glory
        to judge the living and the dead,
        and his kingdom will have no end."

        (AC: "On the third day he rose again.
        He ascended into heaven,
        and is seated at the right hand of the Father.
        He will come again
        to judge the living and the dead.")

    165. The presentation in this section of the Nicene Creed of the exaltation of Christ as a sequence of resurrection, ascension and sitting at the right hand of the Father is particularly indebted to the account in Luke/Acts and became the dominant view in the early Church.

    166. The Creed's statements in this section consist almost entirely of direct and indirect quotations from New Testament texts. The purpose of this selection of central biblical affirmations must be seen in light of the original use of creeds in baptism, i.e. in the context of worship, and of identification with Christ in baptism in his suffering and his glory. The Creed reflects a vision of the "history of salvation", similar to that in earlier and shorter creeds in the Eastern and Western Church, e.g. the Apostles' Creed. This is of particular importance with regard to the statements concerning the second advent of Christ and the final consummation.

b) Biblical witness

167. That Jesus rose from the dead is fundamental to the Christian faith and community (1 Cor. 15:4, 13f., 16f.). In the *Gospels* this message is unfolded in the Easter stories. The event itself is never described, but rather the signs thereof: the rolled away stone, the empty tomb (Matt. 28:1-8; Mark 16:1-8; Luke 24:1-8; John 20:1-2).

168. In the same early confession of faith (1 Cor. 15:3-5), the appearances to the apostles are as much part of its content as is the resurrection itself. In their turn, the Gospel narratives underscore the importance of those appearances (Matt. 28:16-20; Luke 24:13-43; John 20:19-28; 21). Their function is at least twofold.

169. On the one hand, they convince the apostles about the identity of the resurrected Lord who is Jesus himself. This is necessary because of the element of "transformation" involved in the glorified status of the resurrected one. Both the gospels and Acts reflect the dilemma created by this transformation as well as the necessity of overcoming the apostles' doubts concerning the identity of the One who appears with Jesus (Matt. 28:17; Luke 24:25-32; 36-43; John 20:24-28; 21:4-13; Acts 9:5/22:8/ 26:15). This identity is central in the early apostolic message of the resurrection (Acts 2:32).

170. On the other hand, and besides being a confirmation, the appearances function as an invitation to the apostles to spread the "Good News" of the resurrection. All Easter appearances end with a summons to relate the experience: the women are to inform the apostles, and the latter are to evangelize the whole world. The resurrection and the apostolic "sending" are inseparable as is evident from Paul's testimony: his only "proof" that he is an apostle lies in that Jesus, the Risen Lord, appeared to him (Rom. 1:4f.; 1 Cor. 15:7f.; Gal 1:11f.).

171. The reason behind this inter-relation between the Easter appearances and apostleship lies in the fact that the gospel proclaims not only the resurrection as a past happening, but also a the *actual* and *definitive* Lordship of the Risen Christ (Matt. 28:18, 20; Luke 24:49; John 17; 20:21-23; Acts 2:36; Rom. 1:4; 10:9; 1 Cor. 12:3; Phil. 2:11). In other words, the resurrection is inseparable from the exaltation of Jesus at the right hand of God (Phil. 2:9-11; Eph. 1:20-22; Col. 1:18f.; Heb. 1:3; Acts 2:33f.). The last two references reflect the use of the classical passages Ps. 2:7 and Ps. 110:1.

172. The "ascension" into heaven is given a special place in Lukan theology (Luke 24:51; Acts 1:6-11). It also occurs in John 3:13; 6:62; 20:17 and in the early hymn found in 1 Tim. 3:16 (see also Eph. 4:8-10).

173. That the ascension manifests the Lordship of Christ can be seen in the fact that in the Creed the affirmation of the return of Christ in glory as the judge of all follows immediately. This "immediate" sequence of ascension and return in glory is clearly found in Acts 1:9-11. It goes back to early traditional confessions (1 Thess. 1:10; see also 1 Cor. 16:21; Rev. 22:17,20) and teachings (1 Thess. 4:14; 1 Cor. 15:23-26; see also 1 Cor. 11:26).

174. Obviously, the "immediate" sequence of such events set so "far apart" can be perceived only by those who believe that Christ is already glorified. For the world, this glorification will be acknowledged only at its manifestation at his coming as judge. For the world, the *chronos* goes on. For Christians, in Christ it has already reached its end; for them, though they continue to live in this world, the *kairos* of Christ's Lordship has already become a present reality (Rom. 8:11; 2 Cor. 5:1-10; Phil. 3:20f.; Eph. 1:18-20; 2:6; Col. 2:12; 3:1-3; 1 Pet. 1:3-5; see also 1 Cor. 8:5f.).

175. This "new reality" experienced by the Christians is due to the fact that Jesus' resurrection affects their beings and lives. Indeed, Christ the exalted "pours out the Holy Spirit" (Acts 2:33; also Rom. 5:5; 8:9-11) upon those whose "first-born brother" he is (Rom. 8:29; also Col. 1:18); he is the "new/last Adam" (1 Cor. 15:45) and, as such, our new/last image (vv. 46-49). Our "new (mode of) life" is defined by Christ (Gal. 2:19f.; Phil. 1:21; also Rom. 6:11,15-23).

ii. Explication for today

He rose again and ascended into heaven

176. Christians believe and confess that Jesus did not remain in the power of death but was raised from the dead. They acknowledge that the resurrection is the decisive event without which "our preaching is in vain and your faith is in vain" (1 Cor. 15:13-14). And they confess the resurrection of Jesus, and the gift of the Holy Spirit which is intimately connected with it, as the foundation of the life and identity of the Church, as the ground of hope for the whole world, and as God's pledge of eternal life.

Commentary

The mystery of the resurrection has always provoked different interpretations. These should, however, not divide Christians as long as they together confess the reality of the resurrected Jesus.

177. The new life of the Risen One is a present reality. It makes its presence felt in various ways, though in a veiled form. It is the ground of joy as well as of hope. The resurrection of Jesus Christ gives rise to joy which expresses itself in hymns, praise and prayers, in the celebration of the sacraments, in Christian fellowship and in the search for a wider and deeper Christian unity. This joy gives the freedom to share the Good News of Jesus Christ, even in the midst of suffering and in difficult circumstances, in service to the poor, the needy and the sick, and in Christian giving. It is the joyous message of the resurrection that enables Christians to cross all human frontiers and break the barriers that divide us — of class, caste, race, sex, religion and ideology.

178. The resurrection of Jesus Christ also evokes *hope* in us — hope for life on earth as well as life beyond death. For it points to the kingdom of God, which offers the possibility of a new future for the whole of humanity and for each individual. In the light of the resurrection Christians must not capitulate before apparent dead-ends or hopeless situations because the God of the resurrection is present in Christ to offer a new possibility, calling forth life out of death. This hope drives away the fear of death and all evil powers. It refuses to be satisfied with maintaining the status quo of the old humanity, and confronts all oppressive powers that thwart new life. The life that is based on the resurrection of Jesus seeks the well-being of the neighbour and the renewal of the whole human community since it knows that Jesus rose again to be the head and Lord of the new humanity.

179. According to the dominant line in the New Testament witness, resurrection and ascension may be considered as different aspects of the one reality of the Lord's exaltation. The risen Lord went to the Father in order to share in his glory and now to make room for us in his communion with the Father.

He sits at the right hand of the Father

180. At the resurrection and ascension, Christ is exalted by the Father. Because of his obedience he was vindicated by the Father as being one with him in honour and dignity and received the title of *Lord*, that is the title by which God is known in the Scriptures (Phil. 2:10). Because of his obedience, he is now forever associated with the sovereignty of God the Father. And thus, at Pentecost, he is the one who pours out the Holy Spirit, and offers to humanity the gift of salvation (Acts 2:33). Nothing comes from God without him. The Epistle to the Colossians even says that it is through him and for him that God created everything in heaven

and on earth, the visible and invisible things, including spiritual powers and authorities (1:15-20). And he will judge the world.

181. When we affirm Christ as *Lord*, who "sits at the right hand of the Father", we affirm our faith that, in spite of human sin and all its painful consequences, God is and will be victorious over all the forces of evil and over death itself. Even now all powers and masters of this world are subject to his sovereignty (cf. Matt. 20:20ff.; Luke 22:24ff.). The exalted Lord is at work everywhere in the world, even outside the Church, for the sake of his kingdom. This supports and strengthens our confidence in carrying out the missionary task of the Church to announce the lordship of Christ to all the world.

182. We also affirm that just as in his earthly life Christ gave himself to the world and accompanied his disciples with prayer on their behalf, so today he continues to *intercede for us*. Jesus Christ who was raised from the dead, who is at the right hand of God, is our advocate, the high priest who always makes intercession for those who draw near to God through him and who is able for all time to save them. Correspondingly, it is in Christ's name, in and through him, that Christians offer their intercessions to the Father, joining their prayers with his and thus sharing his priestly ministry.

183. The Lordship of Christ demands our response. In the Risen Christ we recognize the servant, the crucified one. He calls us to be his faithful disciples, to continue his ministry of loving service, to take up our cross and to suffer for his sake. In so doing we express our acceptance of the Lordship of Jesus Christ and give our witness to the world. Christians proclaim that the forces of death and evil have been defeated and that Christ now reigns with the Father. This affirmation seems to be in strong contrast to our experience of a world in which we know evil and suffering in many forms, and in which all life ends in death. There is no unambiguous experience of God's kingdom of peace, justice and love in this world. Nevertheless the Christian faith affirms that Jesus Christ even now is Lord and Master of this world. Even the powers of evil and death are made subservient to the purpose of his kingdom.

184. Today we still await the fulfilment of Christ's victory and reign, but with the eyes of faith we see *signs of the new life of the resurrection* present in our midst, wherever this new life breaks into the old. We recognize resurrection signs in the lives of men and women who fearlessly commit themselves to follow the crucified one, and in the witness of the many confessors and martyrs of every age. We experience foretastes of resurrection whenever faith, hope and love in Christ become

manifest in a new sense of community, healing, reconciliation and genuine liberation.

He will come again in glory to judge the living and the dead

185. In proclaiming that "Christ will come again" we affirm our faith that though this world will come to an end, nevertheless God's history with his creation will be brought to a final completion in the One in whom all things had their beginning, the One who is the Alpha and the Omega. We recognize that there is a tension between the inauguration of the kingdom in Christ and its final fulfilment, but we believe that the new creation begun in Christ will also be fulfilled in Christ. We understand this as an all-inclusive *fulfilment*, for our individual justification and salvation is only part of the longed-for redemption of the whole creation. Thus Christians wait in eager hope for the final fulfilment and consummation of God's offer of new life, which is given to our world and history in the resurrection of Christ, the crucified Lord.

186. The coming again of the Lord is believed to be "in glory". That means that he will come triumphantly in the power and authority of God to judge the world but also to grant the faithful the transfiguration of their lives by participating in God's glory so that the promised day of rest will finally be established. In the hope that all will be saved, Christians are confident that the joy of creation and redemption will be fully shared by the faithful followers of Christ.

187. As Christians we are united in our conviction that we all have to appear before the *judgement of Christ*. There are different emphases in the New Testament witness of how the judgement will occur. The proclamation of Christ as the judge needs to be balanced by the recognition that Christ is the advocate who pleads on our behalf as we stand before the Father, and is himself the sacrifice for our sins. But not everything in our present life can survive in the presence of God (cf. 1 Cor. 3:13-15).

Commentary

There are, however, differing opinions about the time and manner of Christ's return and of the judgement. There are some who emphasize a realized eschatology, in which judgement is primarily a present experience, while others have a more apocalyptic understanding, emphasizing the end-time and the judgement yet to come. Some stress an individual resurrection of the dead following the death of each individual; others emphasize the judgement which will occur only with the universal resurrection at the end of time. This diversity of Christian understanding reflects a diversity both in interpretations of the New Testament writings and in these writings themselves.

188. The temptation of Christians is often to set themselves up in judgement of others, or to desire a divine judge who will judge according to *their* will. However we believe that the Good News is that we are not called upon to judge. This does not mean that we are to refrain from creative social criticism and political action. But judgement is *God's prerogative* and will take place according to God's will as revealed in Christ. As such, it may well have outcomes different from those which we expect and desire.

189. As far as God's judgement of us is concerned, we agree in our belief that, however much righteousness and love may be in tension in human life, the full witness of the Bible is that in God they cannot be separated. We are not righteous, but our judge is the righteous One. We cannot abdicate our human responsibility for our sin, but we face our judgement trusting in God's merciful and forgiving love, revealed to us in the Christ who himself has gone through suffering and vindication, and teaches us to love our enemies.

His kingdom will have no end

190. The risen Christ is exalted at the right hand of the Father, wielding the power of his kingdom. Although this will become apparent only at the time of his second coming, the Church affirms it as a reality even now, hidden from our eyes, but nevertheless effective.

Commentary

During the first centuries there were different opinions as to the duration of that kingdom of Christ. The so-called "millenarianists" dreamt of "a thousand years" when, on his second coming, the saints would rule over the world together with Christ. This opinion interpreted Rev. 20:1-6 in the line of Jewish apocalyptic expectations. It also appealed to the apostle Paul who in 1 Cor. 15:28 said that in the end the Son will return his kingdom to the Father. To such an interpretation it seemed that Paul presupposed a period of messianic rule distinct from the eternal kingdom of the Father himself. But the context of this Pauline passage does not support such an interpretation.

191. From the beginning of his earthly mission, Jesus proclaimed the kingdom of the Father (Mark 1:15). His ministry meant that the kingdom of the Father became a present reality among the people, "in their midst" (Luke 17:21; cf. 11:20). Thus his own kingdom can never be anything other than to prepare and bring about the kingdom of the Father. This precisely is his kingdom: to persuade and lead everyone and everything into submission to the Father; just as the Son submits himself to the Father. Christ the king does not seek his own rule, but that of the Father, and therefore his kingdom "will have no end" (Luke 1:33).

Commentary

To confess the kingdom of Christ entails a polemical as well as a constructive relation to the kingdoms and empires of this world. *Polemically*, it implies criticism of systems and ideologies — *Ideologiekritik* — with the unmasking of the false claims to permanence made in every kind of imperialism. World history — even church history — has produced so many "kingdoms" designed to last a "thousand years" or to have "definitive validity" — totalitarian entities, in fact, which have been experiments that were gruesome in their results. In politics the Christian is helped by the sobering yet also encouraging knowledge that only *God's* kingdom — the kingdom of his "righteousness and peace and joy in the Holy Spirit" (Rom. 14:17) — is without end. *Constructively*, the kingdom of God does have relevance for the temporal kingdoms of the world, for, provisional as they are, it provides them with a perspective of their ultimate destiny and with a criterion of what will be expected of them by the coming Judge. World history should be moulded with that judgement in mind — that is, in the light of the kingdom of the *Pantocrator*, the Ruler of all creation.

192. "Beloved, we are God's children now; it does not yet appear what we shall be, but we know that when he appears we shall be like him, for we shall see him as he is" (1 John 3:2).

PART III

We Believe in the Holy Spirit, the Church and the Life of the World to Come

A. THE HOLY SPIRIT

193. The Church confesses and worships the Holy Spirit, "the Lord, the Giver of life". And it is only in the power of the Holy Spirit that Christian faith and its confession are possible. Because the God whom we confess in the Creed is revealed as a Triune God, faith in the Holy Spirit is never to be isolated from faith in the Father and in the Son. In the Church the Holy Spirit is never experienced, confessed or worshipped apart from the Father and the Son. As the Lord and Giver of life, the Holy Spirit enables our communion with the Father and the Son and is, therefore, fundamental to Christian faith, life and hope.

194. Faith in the Holy Spirit is also fundamental to our understanding of the Church, to our confession of one baptism for the remission of sins, and to our expectation of the resurrection of the dead and the life of the world to come.

195. There are many challenges to the confession of the Holy Spirit today. Among them the most pressing are: the conflict between East and West as to the *filioque*; the relation of the divine Spirit to the human spirit, consciousness and conscience; the relation of the Holy Spirit to the prophecy of the Old Covenant and the gift of prophecy in the Church; the criteria for the discernment of the activity of the Spirit within the Church; and the question of the activity of the Spirit outside the Church.

I. The Creed and its biblical witness

a) The text of the Creed

196. "We believe in the Holy Spirit,
the Lord, the Giver of life,

who proceeds from the Father.
Who, with the Father and the Son,
is worshipped and glorified.
Who has spoken through the Prophets."

(AC: "I believe in the Holy Spirit.")

197. When in the Nicene-Constantinopolitan Creed the Fathers of the Church confessed their faith in the Holy Spirit, they were receiving and witnessing the faith transmitted since the apostolic age. They were also influenced in their confession by the questions of several Christian groups relating to the Holy Spirit and even by the denial by some of the divinity of the third person of the Trinity. They were also concerned with clarifying the common faith of the Church which was already confessed either implicitly or in a variety of expressions, especially in the liturgical life. Baptism was administered in the name of the Father, the Son and the Holy Spirit; and in the variety of doxological forms, the Holy Spirit was glorified together with the Father and the Son.

Commentary

The Creed does not call the Holy Spirit "God" as it does the Son when it refers to him as "true God of true God". The Creed does not use, as does later theology, the term *homoousios* to describe the identity of the Holy Spirit in relation to God the Father, as it does to describe the identity of the divinity of the Son in relation to the Father. In using the title "Lord" for the Holy Spirit, however, the Creed affirms that the Spirit's divinity is exactly that of the Father and the Son which was defended through the use of the term *homoousios*. Thereby the Church establishes its doctrine of the Holy Trinity of three divine persons (or *hypostaseis*) — Father, Son and Holy Spirit — in the perfect unity of one and the same divine being *(ousia)*.

b) Biblical witness

198. The first Christian generation affirmed the Holy Spirit as the one by whom Christ was conceived and born of the virgin Mary (Luke 1:35), and who confirmed Jesus in his baptism as Messiah (Matt. 5:16; par. Mark 1:10; Acts 10:38); the Spirit who was present in Christ working through his whole ministry (Matt. 12:28; Luke 4:14; John 1:32f.), and raised him from the dead (1 Cor. 15:45).

The first Christians recognized that this was the same Spirit who in the creation moved over the waters (Gen. 1:2), who spoke through the prophets, anointed the kings of the people, and inspired the prayers of the faithful. The event of Pentecost they experienced, understood, and proclaimed as the pouring out of the same Spirit, who had already spoken through the prophets, as the gift of the final times (Acts 2:1-21). The New Testament shows clearly that the Spirit given at Pentecost is the source of the life of the Church, who in the preaching of the Good News awakens faith and joins new members to the body of Christ through baptism. The Holy Spirit kindles faith (1 Cor. 12:3) and provides the gifts necessary for the life of the believer and the community (1 Cor. 12:4-13; 14:1). The Spirit inspires prayer (Rom. 8:15-16), the liberty of the children of God (Rom. 8:12-16). From the Holy Spirit will come the final resurrection (Rom. 8:11). The Holy Spirit is the "other Paraclete" (John 14:16). At the end of time it is the Spirit who calls the whole creation to fulfilment in the glory of God (Rev. 22:17).

199. While taking up in this way the Old Testament witness to the Spirit of God, the *apostolic Church* realized, in the light of its faith, that the Spirit, active in history, was not an impersonal power. Having perceived that the Logos of God made flesh in Jesus Christ is a person, Christians were enabled to confess in a similar way that the Spirit of God is also a divine person. Consequently, they recognized that the Holy Spirit, together with the Father and the Son, is a divine person active in the economy of salvation (Ps. 33:6; Ezek. 37:1-4; Rom. 1:3-5; 8:14-17).

II. Explication for today

Belief in the Holy Spirit

200. To believe in the Holy Spirit is to affirm that the Holy Spirit is a divine person, always present and active in the Church. Whenever the Father and the Son are at work, there also the Spirit is to be found. The whole of creation and every divine blessing upon it comes from the Father through the Son in the Spirit. And it is in the Spirit and through the Son that the Father is glorified when the world becomes what it ought to be, a sacrifice of praise.

Commentary

Christians differ in their understanding concerning the activity of the Holy Spirit outside the Church. Some would claim it is only within the Christian community that the Spirit of Christ is active. Others would claim that "whatever is true, whatever is honourable, whatever is just" (Phil. 4:8) in the life and actions of those who are not Christians and even of those who do not believe in God, is of God's Holy Spirit, and yet others that the sovereignty of the Spirit in history is hidden from our eyes.

201. The Spirit of God is holy because the Spirit belongs to the eternal being of the Trinity, the totally Other, and acts in the economy of salvation to bring humanity into communion with the Holy being of the Triune God. To have this communion, without which no person can find life and salvation, is a gracious gift of God.

202. *The Holy Spirit* is described in Scripture as God's very breath (cf. John 20:22-23), God's living and life-creating power, truth and love. The Holy Spirit is not one of the many spirits which are supposed to inhabit the universe. The Spirit is opposed to every form of material and spiritual evil. Through the Holy Spirit the created world is sanctified by God's grace. Apart from the Holy Spirit things become carnal and dead.

Commentary

Because God's Spirit *(Ru'ah)* is feminine in Hebrew and related languages, some contend that the Holy Spirit must be considered somehow as a "feminine principle" in God, and referred to as "she". The churches, however, affirm the scriptural imagery with its symbolic analogy and the use of metaphorical language, while retaining the masculine or neuter gender as traditionally used.

The Lord

203. In confessing the Spirit as Lord, the Church acclaims the divinity of the Spirit and acknowledges the lordship of the Spirit over all creation and history. As a divine person the Spirit is one with God the Lord *(Theos Kyrios)*, one with Christ the Lord *(Christos Kyrios)*.

204. The Spirit's *lordship* is not a lordship of brute force, oppressive power or tyrannous manipulation. It is, on the contrary, a lordship which frees all creation and grants "the glorious liberty of the children of God" (cf. Rom. 8:21). Evil spirits possess. Spiritless flesh enslaves. Wicked powers oppress, dominate, manipulate and exploit. The Holy Spirit liberates men and women, even from the most oppressive and enslaving forms of human sin: a power which enables them to resist evil and to struggle towards overcoming it.

The Giver of life

205. Through and in the Spirit of God the gift of life is bestowed on created beings. All forms of life are gifts of God (Ps. 104: 29,30) to be treated with respect: human life as well as that of all other living creatures, the animals, birds of the air and the fish in the sea. Humankind, created in the image and likeness of God, has been given dominion over the created world. However, as God's partners men and women have the duty to respect, defend and preserve the integrity of creation, disrupted by pollution and the exploitation of nature and the violation of human rights, so that God's gift of life may flourish. In the context of modern society there is an urgent need to affirm our responsibility as Christians for the integrity of creation in obedience to the Creator of all.

Commentary

There is need to re-affirm our respect for the integrity of creation while avoiding a sacralization of nature. The Holy Spirit, dwelling in God's creation, gives a quality to the world but the Holy Spirit is neither identical with biological life nor to be identified with human consciousness as was sometimes the case in nineteenth-century philosophy.

But even apart from the pollution and exploitation of nature by human beings, the creation is subjected to futility and to the bondage of decay (Rom. 8:21).

206. The Spirit also gives the new life in Christ: human beings are born anew as the first-fruits of the new creation, and with the rest of creation groan in anticipation (Rom. 8:11,19-20) of the sharing in the new heavens and the new earth. The Spirit in baptism brings to birth new children of the Father — in the one Son, whose own humanity has already been filled with the life of the Spirit. In this way the Spirit in baptism is the source of the Spirit-enlivened Church, the living body of Christ.

207. In creation, redemption and sanctification acting by his Son and Spirit God fills all things and opens his divine life to all. By becoming "partakers of the divine nature" (2 Pet. 1:3-4) believers enter into *communion with the Triune God.* Those who by the power of the Holy Spirit remain "faithful unto death" will receive "the crown of life" (Rev. 2:11).

208. Through the proclamation of the Gospel and the celebration of the sacraments the Holy Spirit is creating and sustaining the faith of God's people. The Spirit pours out an abundance of *charisms.* These charisms

are for the building-up of the Church and for service in the world, through teaching, prophecy, healing, miracles, tongues and the discernment of spirits (1 Cor. 12:4-11,27-30). Since all these gifts are given to individuals for the common good (1 Cor. 12:7) when rightly employed they serve to strengthen the unity of the one body to which we are called in the one baptism (Eph. 4:4-5).

Commentary

There is broad agreement that the gift of the Spirit is inseparable from faith and baptism. However, some churches specifically associate the gift of charism with the sacrament of chrism. Other churches, groups and movements understand the gift of the Spirit to be a separate and distinct work of grace. Hence they look for signs of this gift in special charisms such as speaking in tongues or healing, as the Spirit "completes" the blessing received from God. Although the churches are not yet one in their understanding of the relation of the Spirit's gifts to baptism, all believe that the gifts of the Spirit must not become occasions for church disunity, but are given for the common good of the Church.

Procession from the Father

209. The Holy Spirit "proceeds from the Father". This is the Father from whom the Son is begotten. The affirmation of the procession of the Spirit from the Father includes a profound understanding of the relation between the Father, the Son and the Holy Spirit. The Spirit in the breathing forth and as breathed forth is always in relation to the Son. Therefore, the communion and unity of the Spirit with Christ in the economy of salvation is indissoluble.

210. Despite the controversy created by the introduction of the term *filioque* by Western Christians to express this latter relation, both Western and Eastern Christians have wished to be faithful to the affirmation of the Nicene-Constantinopolitan Creed that the Spirit proceeds from the Father, and both agree today that the intimate relationship between the Son and the Spirit is to be affirmed without giving the impression that the Spirit is subordinated to the Son. On that affirmation all Christians can agree and this enables an increasing number of Western churches to consider using the Creed in its original form.

Commentary

Western Christians have used the term *filioque*, which they introduced into the original text of the Creed as a result of a complicated historical process because they insisted that the procession of the Spirit should not be conceived without a relationship to the Son. Eastern Christians have found most interpretations of its meaning unacceptable and so have stressed that the Spirit proceeds from the Father alone. Thus, Eastern and Western Christians have come to express the one faith they share, even their understanding of the one original Creed they share, in differing ways. On the foundation of this common faith they are now seeking ways to explain these different understandings to each other that are faithful to their original common confession. This process of explaining and learning from each other will take time but it has begun (cf. among others *Spirit of God, Spirit of Christ. Ecumenical Reflections on the Filioque Controversy*, ed. L. Vischer, Faith and Order Paper No. 103, SPCK, London/WCC, Geneva, 1981). As they, through the life-giving power of the Spirit, proceed on this path of mutual understanding, they more and more confess together the Creed in the original form.

211. The Holy Spirit of God, "together with the Father and the Son, is worshipped and glorified", as exemplified in the baptismal confessions, doxologies, liturgical salutations and eucharistic prayers. Along with the intercessions for the children of the Father, made through Christ, the glory and praise to the Triune God is the most basic aspect of Christian prayer — a prayer animated by the Holy Spirit. Spirituality is only fully and maturely Christian when it is Trinitarian. So Christians in their daily life and especially in their worship pray that the Father send his Spirit that they might be more completely conformed to the life of Christ the Son (cf. Rom. 8:29).

212. In turn Christians reject any claims about the activity of the Holy Spirit in the lives of individuals or communities which would suggest that the Spirit acts independently of the Father or the Son. All churches are convinced that, together with the Father and the Son, the Holy Spirit is active in the revelation of God's design and his saving action. Similarly because they also believe that the Holy Spirit is the life-centre of each Christian, every time they praise and glorify God they praise the Holy Spirit with the Father and the Son. Furthermore, some churches which have not placed much emphasis on *Trinitarian spirituality*, or prayer for the gift and action of the Holy Spirit *(epiklesis)*, are now rediscovering this dimension of Christian life and worship. It is a Christian custom to begin and end worship services in the name and with the blessing of the

Father, the Son and the Holy Spirit. Christians, therefore, glorify the Triune God through prayer, common worship and the daily service which is their acceptable sacrifice (cf. Rom. 12:1f.).

The Spirit and the prophets

213. The Holy Spirit "has spoken through the prophets". In this affirmation the Church, which is in continuity with the people of God of the Old Covenant and is at the same time indeed the people of God of the New Covenant, insists that God's Spirit is the same Spirit who inspired both the *prophets of Israel* and the canonical Hebrew scriptures. The Jewish people have continued through the centuries, on the basis of their tradition, to listen and to respond to God's Spirit speaking through these scriptures. Christians, likewise, continued to be taught by the Spirit through the prophets, as understood in the light of the revelation of Christ (John 5:39). In this, hope is given that the Spirit of God will draw both communities closer together by his continuing activity (Rom. 11:29-32).

> *Commentary*
>
> The confession that the Holy Spirit "spoke through the prophets" rejects any position among Christians, whether in the past or in the present, which would deny that the God of the prophets is the same God as the Father of Jesus Christ. In our time many Christians have been led to reconsider the traditional attitude of the Church towards the people of Jewish faith. It is recognized that the Hebrew prophets announced an eschatological coming of a Messiah who above all would renew the face of the earth. In view of the fulfilment of this proclamation Jesus is understood by Christians as the Messiah. Christians and Jews might be able to come nearer to each other by studying their respective eschatological expectations of God's final kingdom and by seeking ways of common service to humankind in this perspective.

214. Christians believe that Jesus is the fulfilment of Old Testament prophecy and is himself God's anointed prophet upon whom the Holy Spirit rested in a definitive way. Through the mission of the Spirit, sent by the risen Lord from the Father, the gift of prophecy was transmitted to the Church. Everything the Holy Spirit inspires is bound to what God the Father has done in his Spirit-filled Christ.

215. The affirmation of the Creed that the Spirit spoke through the prophets does not deny the Christian belief and experience that the *gifts of*

prophecy are still bestowed today. These gifts are expressed in manifold ways; in those who proclaim a specific word of God in situations of oppression and injustice and also by those who edify the Church in its worship service and by those who in some churches are involved in forms of charismatic renewal. The suffering of prophetic witnesses will always be part of the Church's life and service to the world. "The blood of the martyrs is the seed of the Church." Not everyone who claims prophetic gifts, however, is necessarily inspired by the Holy Spirit. The gift of discernment remains to be exercised by believers since "the spirits of prophets are subject to prophets" (1 Cor. 14:32; cf. also 14:22). The confession of Jesus Christ as Lord, according to the apostle Paul, serves as the decisive criterion for distinguishing the Spirit of God from other prophetic spirits (1 Cor. 12:3). In the history of the Church additional criteria drawn from the biblical witness and the tradition and confession of the Church have been employed as required by specific situations and challenges (cf. for example 1 John 4:2-3).

B. ONE, HOLY, CATHOLIC AND APOSTOLIC CHURCH

216. Christians believe and confess with the Creed that there is an indissoluble link between the work of God in Jesus Christ through the Holy Spirit and the *reality* of the Church. This is the testimony of the Scriptures. The origin of the Church is rooted in the plan of the Triune God for humankind's salvation. The New Testament connects the event of its manifestation with Pentecost. The Church has its basis in the ministry of Christ himself who proclaimed the kingdom of God in word and deed, called men and women and sent them out, empowered by the Holy Spirit (John 20:19-23), to proclaim the same message.

Commentary

The Lima document on *Baptism, Eucharist and Ministry* implies an ecclesiology not explained in an explicit way in the text itself. The Faith and Order programme on *The Unity of the Church and the Renewal of Human Community* includes a reflection on "The Church as Mystery and Prophetic Sign"[1]. In what follows this is explicated more fully, in accordance with the Creed, what we mean by "the Church".

---

[1] Cf. *Church and World. The Unity of the Church and the Renewal of Human Community*, a Faith and Order Study Document, Faith and Order Paper No. 151, WCC, Geneva, 1990.

217. The Creed's emphasis on the Church as the place of the saving action of the Holy Spirit has to face many *challenges*, the most important of which are the following:

— Those who seek Jesus outside the Church deny the relevance of the Church for their own salvation.
— Among others who belong to the Church the necessity of complying with the rules of their community is felt to be an irrelevant burden.
— Others who accept the Church nevertheless contest the exercise of authority that constrains their freedom and deplore the lack of genuine community and mutuality.
— In many churches some forms of charismatic and other movements, because of their feeling of immediacy to God, reject any kind of human authority; others, on the contrary, rely blindly on arbitrary human authority.
— In the eyes of many the division within and between the churches destroys the credibility of the teaching of any of these churches.
— Even among committed Christians the apparent inability of the churches to overcome their historic divisions seems to demonstrate that either the leadership of the churches is not authentically committed to the will of Christ for unity among his disciples or that his commandment itself is an impossible dream.
— In the judgment of the world the meagreness of the fruits of sanctification exhibited by Christians and the failure of Christianity in 2000 years of its history to change profoundly the condition of the world, discredit the claim of the churches.

I. The Creed and its biblical witness

a) The text of the Creed

218. "We believe in one holy catholic and apostolic Church."

(AC: "I believe... the holy catholic Church,
the communion of saints.")

Commentary

With reference to the word "in" see para. 5 and commentary.

219. The sequence in the third article of the Creed moves from belief in the Holy Spirit to belief in the Church. This indicates the close relationship of the Church's reality to the work of the Spirit. It prevents the Church from appearing as an isolated object of faith.

220. The Creed identifies the Church as one, holy, catholic and apostolic. This is the richest form of confessing the Church in the history of early Christian creeds. It begins with the oneness which had a special relevance in the face of the divisions of the fourth century. Its holiness refers to the fundamental fact that the Church belongs to the Holy One and is called to fidelity. Its catholicity means that it is the gift of God for all people whatever their particular country, race, social condition or language, that is to say for the whole *oikoumene* as understood at the time of the Council of Constantinople. The apostolicity of the Church expresses its obligation and commitment to the norm of the apostolic gospel of God's action in the cross and resurrection of Jesus Christ.

b) Biblical witness

221. The New Testament uses several images in speaking of the Church (vine, temple, building, bride, the new Jerusalem, the people of God). Each has its own significance. Particular attention, however, has been given to the Church as body of Christ. This is more than an image because the term refers to the fundamental reality of the participation in the body of Christ in the eucharist as constitutive, through the Spirit, of the communion (koinonia) among all those who partake in the Lord's supper (1 Cor. 10:16-17 and 11:23-30). Wherever in the Pauline literature the expression *Body of Christ* occurs (Rom. 12:4-5; 1 Cor. 12:12-27; Eph. 1:22-23), this profound association is implied. It underlines the intimate, organic relationship which exists between the Risen Lord and all those who receive the new life through communion in him.

222. The Church has been built on the foundation of the apostles and prophets, Jesus Christ being himself the cornerstone (Eph. 2:20). It has its origin in Christ's proclamation of the kingdom of God and in the history of his crucifixion and resurrection. It became manifest in the meals Jesus celebrated, especially in his last supper (Luke 22:7-20). According to Acts, at Pentecost the Church received the power of the Holy Spirit for its life and mission (Acts 2:1-13). It spreads the good news of God's saving action in Jesus Christ to reconcile the world to himself (2 Cor. 5:18-19).

223. The New Testament takes up and elaborates the Old Testament concept of the election of Israel, "a chosen race, a royal priesthood, a holy nation, God's own people" (1 Pet. 2:9; cf. Ex. 19:6 Septuagint (LXX)) in extending it to the Church. Thus the *ecclesia* of the New Covenant is linked to the beginning and model of the people of God in the *qahal* of the old. The Church is called to declare "the wonderful deeds of

him who called you out of the darkness into his marvellous light" (1 Pet.
2:9). According to Paul the election of the Church of God in Jesus
Christ does not undo the election of Israel, though only in the eschaton
all of Israel, the remnant of which became the core of the Church of
Christ, will be reunited with the Church in the one people of God (Rom.
11:1-36).

II. Explication for today

The Church and the Trinitarian communion

224. The Church is the community of those who are in communion
with Christ and, through him, with one another. Each of its members
enters into this communion through faith in Christ and the one baptism for
the forgiveness of sins. It is a community of those who desire to persevere
by the power of the Spirit in a life nourished by the word of God and the
eucharist. They are consecrated to the witness and service of the gospel in
a communion of love through the Spirit of Jesus Christ. Since the Church
in its historical and human reality constantly fails to correspond to its
divine vocation, it is constantly recalled and empowered by God to a
renewal of its life and mission.

225. The life and unity of the Church are grounded in the communion
of the Trinity. The Father willed it as the people of his possession, the
Son redeems and offers it as his living Body, the Spirit gathers it into a
unique communion. Thus the Church is "the people united by the unity of
the Father and the Son and the Holy Spirit".[2]

226. This community finds its full manifestation wherever people are
gathered together by word and sacrament in obedience to the apostolic
faith — i.e. in a local church. All local churches and their members
should enjoy unity in the same faith and life, reflecting the Trinitarian
communion of the Father, Son and Holy Spirit. Each local church is
authentically the Church of God, when all it preaches, celebrates and does
is in communion with all that the churches in communion with the
apostles preached, celebrated and did, and with all that the churches here
and now are preaching, celebrating and doing in communion with the
apostles and under the apostolic gospel. In this way the universal Church
consists in the communion of local churches. However, as long as
ecclesial divisions exist, the presence of the one Church of Christ
continues to be diminished in each of them.

---

[2] Cyprian, *De Orat. Dom.* 23.

Commentary

Sometimes Christians have difficulties in receiving each other's statements about the Church because they understand and use the word "Church" differently.

In the Eastern Christian tradition the Church is predominantly seen in terms of the divine mystery of being-the-Church so that the perfection of the Church, known only by faith, dominates the orientation and renders it practically meaningless to speak of a church sinful, imperfect, in need of change, etc.

In the Western churches it is more common to link statements of faith and historical reality — the Church as divine mystery, and the Church as a fragile human community — in a dialectical language of divine and human, thus expressing the tension of faith and historical reality in one unified conceptuality.

The difference certainly implies less substantial theological disagreement than it immediately seems to do. However, the question remains whether it indicates some wide-ranging difference in the basic direction of ecclesiological vision.

The Church, the Body of Christ

227. When the New Testament speaks of the Church as the Body of Christ, it underlines the basic importance of his incarnation, passion and resurrection (his bodiliness) for the salvation of the world. This recalls the constitutive role of the sacraments for Christians: of baptism which integrates human beings into the body of Christ (1 Cor. 12:13) and of the holy communion which constantly renews the life of believers within the Body of Christ (1 Cor. 10:16). The veritable fruit of salvation, *communion*, renewed and re-established between God and humankind, between humans and the world of creation, is brought about and is manifested by the holy mystery of the Body of Christ.

228. The Church is Christ's living Body. It exists in local congregations and worldwide communion with each other. It is particular in its difference from the world and inclusive in its mission to the world. It is called to serve the Lord through the *diversity* of its members. Together, the royal priesthood of all the faithful and the diverse ordained ministries serve God in the Body of Christ by the Holy Spirit. The Church thus manifests the active presence of the Triune God in the world.

229. The Church is the community of those whom Christ receives at his table and who give thanks to the Triune God in worship and service. It receives the Word of God and celebrates the sacraments, especially the

eucharist (Lord's Supper) which was instituted by Jesus Christ himself. It is called to praise God for all his creation, to worship and pray on behalf of itself and the world. It is called to serve all people in the name of Jesus (cf. Matt. 25:31ff.).

230. As Christ is given by the Father *for* and *to* humankind, so the Church as Christ's body is sent into the world. The gift for which the Church continually gives thanks unites the vision of the reign of God over all creation with the uniqueness of Christ's incarnation, death, resurrection and ascension. At the same time it enables Christians to understand the inter-relatedness and unity of "leitourgia" and "diakonia". The community is contemplative and active, serving God and humankind, and it will remain so until the end of time when it will be taken up into the all-embracing and all-restoring kingdom of God.

The Church, the communion of saints in the Spirit

231. Although the phrase "the communion of saints" does not occur in the Nicene Creed, nevertheless it is associated with belief in the Church and specifically mentioned in the Apostles' Creed. This communion unites the faithful of every age and of all places in one fellowship of prayer, praise and of sharing in suffering and joy. The Church is such a communion because all those who believe in Christ are in one true fellowship with the Father and his Son, Jesus Christ, and by partaking of the same divine gift are united together in the Holy Spirit (1 John 1:3).

It is the communion of saints because all are baptized in Christ, who is the Holy One, though Christians stand in need of repentance and daily forgiveness. It is the Holy Spirit who strengthens and renews God's holy community through word and sacramental life for service, thanksgiving and praise.

232. All ages, including our own, contribute to the hosts of *witnesses* and martyrs who in their sufferings "complete what is lacking in Christ's afflictions for the sake of his body, that is, the Church" (Col. 1:24). Their suffering with and for Jesus Christ obliges the whole Church to participate with them in solidarity and intercession (2 Tim. 2:11-13).

233. The Church is the *prefiguration of the kingdom* which it expects and announces. The gospel it proclaims and the witness it renders invite all people to accept the Good News of the kingdom. It cannot be subject to the realities of this world always at work in its members, since it is orientated towards the coming kingdom which it proclaims in word and deed, and which it already experiences. It awaits the glorious return of Christ, its Lord, an expectancy which it expresses most vigorously in its

liturgy. Every time two or three disciples of Christ are united, the Lord himself is present in their midst anticipating the kingdom (cf. Matt. 18:20).

The Church, the people of God

234. In the Scriptures, the Church is called the people of God. This means that the Church exists *in continuity* with the Old Testament people of God and inherits the promises given to it. However, as people of God, the Church also exists *in a certain discontinuity* with the Old Testament people of God (cf. para. 223). This shows that God's purpose of salvation in electing a people has an ongoing history. Therefore the Church itself is a pilgrim people which is led by the Triune God to the promised future (in an earlier period this was expressed by the terms *ecclesia militans* and *ecclesia triumphans*).

235. The Church, as the people of God, is a community of women and men of all ages, races, cultures, social and economic backgrounds who are made members of the body by God through faith and baptism. Those who truly belong to the people of God are known to God alone. Therefore, the boundaries of the Church will be revealed not before the Last Day when all hidden things become visible.

236. As people of God, the Church belongs in the mystery of God's economy of salvation which has been revealed in Jesus Christ. Therefore, in a certain sense the Church, in celebrating the presence of Christ, can be included in the word "mystery". At the same time the Church is a prophetic sign because the execution of God's plan of salvation has not yet reached its final completion. As prophetic sign it is the means of God's active and transforming presence in the world.[3] In proclaiming the word of God and celebrating the sacraments, the Church does not only exist for itself, but also for the world God desires. It is not a fortress in which people can enclose themselves for a life of security, but a servant people spread throughout the world, sent in missionary outreach to sow the good seed of the word and to bring Christ's love to all people.

237. The Church, as the people of God, rejoices in all the signs of the caring work of the Creator which it encounters in the world, in all truth, beauty and goodness. It is also called to recognize the brokenness of the world and the sinfulness of humankind including its own. It offers thanks to God for his goodness and intercedes for the brokenness of the world

---

[3] Cf. *Church — Kingdom — World. The Church as Mystery and Prophetic Sign*, ed. G. Limouris, Faith and Order Paper No. 130, WCC, Geneva, 1986, Chapters III and IV.

and repents of its own unfaithfulness. It trusts in God who grants forgiveness and will restore all things in a new creation. Thus, in a world continously distorted by sin and the powers of evil, the Church exists as a sign of God's loving purpose for the world even when it but poorly responds to its calling.

One, holy, catholic and apostolic Church

238. As there is one Lord and one Spirit, there is but *one Church*, one faith and one baptism. All the baptized are incorporated into one body which is called to witness to its one and only Saviour. Christians are called to manifest the unity they have in Christ by their oneness in the apostolic faith and in the sacramental life. In attesting the one gospel, the one baptism, the one faith expressed in the Creeds of the ancient Church, the sharing of the one mission implying communion in one ministry and common prayer, the Scriptures point towards this visible unity which can be fully actualized only in one eucharistic communion. This unity does not imply uniformity, but an organic bond of unity among all the local churches comprising the richness of their diversities.

239. The Holy Spirit dwells in the *holy church*. This Church has been set apart by God who is holy and who sanctifies it by the word and sacraments. The holiness of the Church signifies the faithfulness of God towards his people: the gates of hell will not prevail against it. Even at the darkest times in the Church's history, Christ continues to justify and sanctify those who remain faithful so that the Church even in such times is able to render its service for the salvation of humankind. It is also holy because of the holy words it proclaims and the holy acts it performs. Though it is a community of sinners, aware that God's judgement begins with them (1 Pet. 4:17), it is holy because it is sustained by the knowledge that they have been and are constantly being forgiven. In spite of the sin in the Church, when it celebrates the eucharist and listens to the word of God it is seized by the Holy One and cleansed.

240. Christ, full of grace and truth, is already present on earth in the *Church catholic*. In each local church the fullness of grace and truth is present — a catholicity which requires the communion of all local churches and which pertains to the identity of each local church and constitutes an essential quality of their communion together. This catholic nature of the Church is realized and expressed in a great diversity of Christian spiritual life and witness among all peoples in space and time. This catholicity transcends nationalism, particular traditions and all human barriers. It is a fullness of life. In the life of the Church the whole

human being and all human situations are enlisted for the worship and the service to God in the diversity of rites and traditions. In the worship of each local church the whole mystery of Christ is present. Where Jesus Christ is, there too is the Church catholic, in which in all ages the Holy Spirit makes people participants of Christ's life and salvation, without respect of sex, race of position.

241. The *church* is *apostolic* because everything it confesses about Christ comes from the apostles as witness, whose testimony to the life, death and resurrection of Jesus Christ has been transmitted by the Holy Scripture. In this continuity the Church recognizes and lives its fundamental identity with the Church of Christ's apostles on which it is built once and for all.

The *apostolicity* of the Church is manifested in its faithfulness to the word of God, lived out and witnessed to in the apostolic Tradition, guided by the Holy Spirit throughout the centuries, and expressed in the ecumenical Creed. It is manifested in its celebration of the sacraments, through the continuity of its ministry in the service of Christ and his Church in communion with the apostles and through the committed Christian life of all its members and communities.

The Church is *apostolic* by following the example of the apostles in continuing their mission to proclaim the gospel which is confirmed by the action and the gift of the Holy Spirit. It witnesses to and serves the reconciliation of humankind to God in Jesus Christ. In obedience to the mandate of Jesus Christ the Church proclaims the divine salvation to the world. In so doing it also announces the divine judgment on sin revealed in the cross set in a hostile world, whose powers are still threatening, even though they have been broken in the victory of Christ. This victory calls forth from the Church a response of conscious self-emptying, the stripping of itself of any exalted status so that, motivated by sacrificial love, it remains the servant of Christ's mission in the world until he comes again in glory.

Thus the Church can fulfil its mission to the world only in so far as it is itself continuously renewed as the one, holy, catholic and apostolic Church.

Commentary

The various Christian traditions differ in their understanding of *apostolic succession*. Some put the emphasis on succession in apostolic teaching. Others combine this with the recognition of an ordered transmission of the ministry of word and sacrament. Others again understand apostolic succession primarily as the unbroken succession of episcopal ordinations.

In ecumenical dialogues there is a growing agreement that the apostolicity or *apostolic tradition* of the Church is broader than the concept of apostolic succession of ministry, which is a part and sign of that apostolic tradition which it serves. The question as to whether episcopal succession is the most adequate expression of apostolic succession and continuity in the apostolic mission of the Church is now at the centre of the ecumenical discussion on ministry.[4]

C. ONE BAPTISM FOR THE FORGIVENESS OF SINS

242. The Church is a communion with Christ himself, through the Spirit, to the glory of the Father. Therefore, the sacrament of baptism, by which God receives the baptized as members of this communion, is acknowledged as the means through which God gives to the faithful the assurance of their participation in the mystery of salvation. They share in the covenant with God, in what happened to Jesus Christ in his death and his resurrection, in the gift of the Spirit at Pentecost; they believe that they will share fully in the life of the world to come.

243. A substantial *challenge* is made to this confession by the fact that in contrast to the one baptism enunciated in the Creed many churches, while officially recognizing each other's baptism, still cannot join together in the celebration of baptism. Furthermore, there are churches which do not recognize the baptism administered by other churches, and some of them practise what appears to be re-baptism when people come over to them. Others question or even reject the practice of infant baptism. A further challenge is whether the Spirit of God, forgiveness of sins and membership in the people of God can be granted only through baptism.

Commentary

For this part C. see the Baptism section in *Baptism, Eucharist and Ministry* and Chap. IV.A of *Baptism, Eucharist and Ministry 1982-1990*, Faith and Order Paper No. 149, WCC, Geneva 1990.

---

[4] Cf. e.g. *Baptism, Eucharist and Ministry* (BEM), Faith and Order Paper No. 111, WCC, Geneva, 1982, Ministry IV, paras 34-38.

I. The Creed and its biblical witness

a) The text of the Creed

244. "We confess one baptism for the forgiveness of sins."

(AC: "I believe ... the forgiveness of sins")

245. The use of the term "acknowledge" *(homologoumen)* here indicates that baptism belongs to the confession of faith, but not in the same way as the three persons of the Trinity in whom we "believe" *(pisteuomen eis)*. The Church acknowledges only one unrepeatable baptism, which is inseparably connected with the confession of faith in God Father, Son and Holy Spirit.

246. Baptism is the only sacrament of the Church mentioned in the Creed, and it is closely related to the forgiveness of sins. The background to this connection is that in the early Church baptism was considered as the occasion when our sinful life is radically transformed by a rebirth to a new life which liberates us from our former sinful nature. It is, of course, true that already at an early date the Church created the possibility of a second conversion and instituted its older sacrament of penance (which was at first public). Besides this, the institution of private confession developed. At a later time it was recognized that the forgiveness of sins is received once for all fundamentally in baptism and that the subsequent occurrences of penance represent a re-appropriation of baptism.

b) Biblical witness

247. Jesus submitted himself to John's baptism of repentence for the forgiveness of sins (Mark 1:4) in order "to fulfil all righteousness" (Matt. 3:15). Jesus' baptism took place as an act of solidarity with sinners; in it the Son heard the voice of the Father and the Spirit descended upon him (Mark 1:10 and par.). It led Jesus on to the path of the Suffering Servant (cf. Mark 10:38-40). This became the model for Christian baptism (Rom. 6:3-6) which began only after Easter. The Risen Christ's command to baptize was passed on in the tradition (Matt. 28:19f.; Mark 16:16).

In the *Old Testament* circumcision was the sign of the covenant of God with his people (in which all the members of Israel were included) (cf. Gen. 17:11-14). References to the saving experience of the people of Israel (e.g. passage through the Red Sea) are used in some cases in the New Testament in connection with baptism (e.g. 1 Cor. 10:1f.), while the fundamental pattern for the understanding of baptism is found in the death and resurrection of Jesus.

248. In the *New Testament* it is by baptism that believers are made members of Christ and his Church. Buried with Christ in baptism they will also live with him because of his resurrection (Rom. 6:1-11; Col. 2:11-12). To confess baptism into Christ is to confess that through Christ who died for our sins we receive assurance of a share in his resurrection (Rom. 8:9-11), together with the forgiveness of sins and the gift of the Holy Spirit. This confidence implies the hope that in the eschatological fulfilment those who have been baptized and believe will be citizens of the New Jerusalem (Rev. 21:1-4) and partakers of the life of the world to come.

The New Testament unfolds the meaning of baptism in various images which express the riches of this sacrament. Baptism is a washing away of sin (1 Cor. 6:11); a new birth (John 3:5); an enlightenment by Christ (Eph. 5:14); a reclothing in Christ (Gal. 3:27); a renewal by the Spirit (Tit. 3:5); the experience of salvation from the flood (1 Pet. 3:20-21); an exodus from bondage (1 Cor. 10:1-2); and a liberation into a new humanity in which barriers of divisions whether of sex or race or social status are transcended (Gal. 3:27-28; 1 Cor. 12:13).

II. Explication for today

One baptism

249. The Christian churches confess "one baptism" as *incorporation into the Body of Christ* — the one Church — taking place once for all. The unity of baptism which is attested to in the Creed reminds us of the "one" Lord Jesus Christ. The "one" baptism, the "one" Lord and the "one" Spirit (cf. Eph. 4:4-5) calls the churches to confess the "one" faith in common and to mutually recognize each other as churches notwithstanding their different forms of life. Through baptism all members of the congregation are called to the one "royal priesthood" (1 Pet. 2:9) of all believers and so to share responsibility in the entire Church and in its mission to the world.

250. In various contexts the relationship between baptism and membership in the Church needs further clarification, especially in the light of the following situations. There are baptized persons who drift away from the life of the Church, not taking part in its activities. There are other baptized persons who, dismayed at the condition of the churches, deliberately separate themselves from the institutional Church for the sake of their own faith and the dignity of their baptism. And there are persons who have not been baptized, but who nevertheless participate actively in

the life of the Church. All these cases raise, in different ways, the question of the relation between baptism and church membership. The true Church is not simply identical with the number of baptized persons, and the actual institutional church suffers (in every denomination) from many kinds of distortion. Nevertheless this must not lead to an underestimation of baptism. All those who have been baptized and even those who have deliberately separated themselves from the Church remain under its care. The Church also has the responsibility of leading to baptism those who have been moved by the gospel but have not yet had their faith sealed by baptism.

251. The one baptism is administered by water with the promise of the Spirit to be given to those who receive baptism according to Jesus' word: "Unless one is born of water and the Spirit he cannot enter the kingdom of God" (John 3:5).

For the forgiveness of sins

252. By its strong emphasis on baptism as the sacrament for the remission of sins, the Creed exhorts us to take our baptism seriously as essentially linked to the beginning of a new life, the *decisive and fundamental change* in our life history that occurs once and for all. In addition, the affirmation of the Creed reminds us that even later repentance, confession and absolution should be considered in relation to our baptism, as a re-appropriation of what happened once and for all in our baptism. In this way baptism is to be taken seriously not simply as a passing ceremony, but rather one that provides the basis for the continuity of the Christian life, within the communion of the family of God (cf. Eph. 2:19).

Commentary

Within the ecumenical community there remain differences about the practice of baptism. For example, according to the ancient tradition of the Church the sacrament of baptism is linked with chrismation and the eucharist. Later, chrismation/eucharist was assigned in parts of the Church to a later point in the initiation process. Differences also still exist as to how traditions discern what is effected in the act of baptism. All are agreed that in baptism by water, conferred in the name of the Father, Son and Holy Spirit, there is the activity of God and the response of the baptized. All are agreed that the activity of God is grace in action and that the human response is faith in action. No one denies that prior to baptism God has acted graciously and the human response has begun to be one of faith.

Differences begin to emerge when the attempt is made to answer the question more precisely as to what it is that God's grace effects in baptism when it is met by the human response of faith. Some take the view that in baptism there is the moment when God's grace effects the remission of sins and that baptism is essentially linked with the beginning of a new life, thus defining baptism as the moment of new birth. Others say that the moment of rebirth when there comes an acceptance by faith of the saving grace of God is prior to baptism. Thus the essential linking of baptism with new life means that the occasion of baptism signifies what has already occurred through God's grace.

How far apart are these two views? Traditionally they have been described as taking either a sacramental or a symbolic view of baptism. Has polarization perhaps produced something of a distortion of both views? Is there not, perhaps, the possibility of a way between what appears to some to be a purely symbolic view on the one hand and to others a seemingly quasi-mechanical understanding of sacramental grace on the other? If all can accept that God has already been acting graciously in some way to bring the person to baptism, if all can acknowledge that the act of baptism itself is an effective sign of God's grace evoking the response of our faith within the Church and that God continues after baptism to act graciously towards the baptized, then the remaining differences need no longer be taken as contradictory.

253. The gift of God granted in baptism requires in every instance the human *response of faith* if it is to impart reconciliation effectively. This is true in every case also for those who are not yet able to answer for themselves. Here we are thinking first of all of the faith of the community within which the baptism takes place, but also of the future faith of baptized persons once they have grown up. In the case of the baptism of those who can answer for themselves, no one denies that God has already acted graciously before their baptism and that their response has already begun to be a response of faith. In both cases baptism itself is an efficacious sign of God's grace evoking the life-long response of faith. The administration of baptism within the worship of the congregation also reminds its members of their own baptism and of its continuing blessing and obligation.

254. Baptism means *participating* in the life, death and resurrection of Jesus Christ. By baptism, Christians are immersed in the liberating death of Christ where their sins are buried, where the "old Adam" is crucified with Christ, and where the power of sin is broken. Christians continue to pray every day "forgive us our trespasses" and to live every day in confidence of their justification. In this sense those baptized are no longer slaves to sin, but free. Fully identified with the death of Christ, they are buried with him and are raised here and now to a new life in the power of the resurrection of Jesus Christ, confident that they will ultimately be one with him in a resurrection like his (Rom. 6:3-11; Col. 2:13; 3:1; Eph. 2:5-6).

Commentary

In the sixteenth century the question of justification divided the Western Church. Martin Luther saw in the Church of his time a thinking and practice which made the grace of God dependent on religious works. In his eyes this was a fundamental matter contrary to the gospel of Jesus Christ. The Catholic side feared that the Reformation theologians and communities, in emphasizing the forensic (juridical) character of justification, neglected the necessity of a new life as a fruit of grace and faith. In the light of common listening to the Holy Scriptures, however, we are today confessing with one another that we are justified without merit by faith alone, that the grace of God also transforms the human being and that Christian life is without credibility if there is no kind of renewal. We confess also with one another that the question of justification concerns the centre of the Christian faith. In light of these insights we can say that the condemnations of the sixteenth century are no more adequate to describe the partner in dialogue of today.

The doctrine of justification has never been a fact of division between the Eastern and Western Christianity. Nevertheless some Orthodox theologians suspected some of the formulations of the Western doctrine as one-sided and too forensic. On the other hand, to Western eyes, the Orthodox doctrine of deification *(theosis)* does not seem to take seriously enough the continuing sinfulness of Christians.

But Orthodox make clear that *theosis* does not imply that human beings become divine in their nature, but rather describes the renewal and rebirth of human beings as well as the illumination and participation of humanity in the divine life through the Holy Spirit. Today Eastern and Western theologians can say that Christians are justified in turning to a new direction which leads them to become "partakers of the divine nature" (2 Pet. 1:4). By this is understood a process by which there is a growth in holiness so that human beings come closer and closer to God. It does not mean that Christians are no longer sinners and in need of daily forgiveness.

255. In baptism God anoints the baptized with the Holy Spirit, marks them with the seal of permanently belonging to Christ and implants in their hearts the first instalment of their inheritance as sons and daughters of God. The Holy Spirit nurtures the life of faith in their hearts until they enter into their eternal heritage (Eph. 1:13-14). The baptism which makes Christians partakers of the mystery of Christ's death and resurrection implies confession of sin and conversion of heart. Thus those baptized are pardoned, cleansed and sanctified by Christ, and are given a *new ethical orientation*, under the guidance of the Holy Spirit, as part of their baptism. The Holy Spirit calls them and motivates them both to personal sanctification and to engaging themselves in every sphere of life for the implementation of God's will.

Commentary

While the early Church administered the anointment (chrism/ confirmation, chrismation) of the baptized as part of the baptismal rite, and the Orthodox churches still continue to do so, the Western Church for various reasons came to turn the act of anointment into an act on its own (confirmation).

256. Baptism is related not only to momentary experience, but to *life-long growth into Christ*. Those baptized are called upon to reflect the glory of the Lord as they are transformed by the power of the Holy Spirit into his likeness, with ever increasing splendour (2 Cor. 3:18). The life of the Christian is necessarily one of continuing struggle, yet also of continuing experience of grace. In this new relationship, the baptized live for the sake of Christ, of his Church and of the world which he loves, while they wait in hope for the manifestation of God's new creation and for the time when God will be all in all. As they grow in the Christian life of faith, baptized believers demonstrate that humanity can be regenerated and liberated.

D. THE RESURRECTION OF THE DEAD
AND THE LIFE OF THE WORLD TO COME

257. The last words of the Creed are about hope. Indeed, Christians are people of hope, the Church is a communion of hope. Empowered by the Holy Spirit, Christians have the assurance that in Christ and his resurrection, God has opened up for them a future and a hope which looks beyond the vicissitudes and predicaments of this time, life and world. Yet this transcendent hope already now becomes a source of strength, perseverance and expectation and is able to bear fruit in the way people live and act.

258. This transcendent expectation and hope faces *challenges* in a world in which resurrections do not happen, where the reality of death seems to be an ultimate fact to which people have to adjust. The message of hope in a life beyond our time and world is confronted by the massive experience of hopelessness in a world haunted by threats of over-population, ecological collapse and the misery of millions. How can these challenges be turned into words and acts of promise?

I. The Creed and its biblical witness

a) The text of the Creed
259. "We look for the resurrection of the dead,
and the life of the world to come. Amen."

(AC: "the resurrection of the body,
and the life everlasting. Amen.")

260. The Creed ends with an eschatological statement which is closely related to the second article of faith. There the emphasis was on the future of Christ, here it is on the future of believers and of a world which is to come. What has to be said about the last judgement of the living and the dead has been stated in the second article and is not repeated in the third article.

261. When the Creed talks of the "resurrection of the dead", a future for believers beyond death is envisaged which is not simply a spiritual future. As distinct from Gnostic and Manichaean ideas, a holistic process affecting body, mind and spirit of human beings is implied.

262. The Apostles' Creed speaks of belief in "life everlasting". When the Nicene-Constantinopolitan Creed refers to the life of the world (or age) to come, it therefore stresses the qualitative difference between the present life and the future life.

b) Biblical witness

263. For the most part the *Old Testament* has little to say about life after death. The realm of the dead is a place of shadows from which no one returns (2 Sam. 12:23); a place without light (Jes. 10:21); a place where no one praises God (Ps. 6:5; 30:9; 115:17). The prophets looked forward to a new age, a future time of blessing and peace, when a new David would reign in Jerusalem (Isa. 9 and 11). In time this future hope became detached from the present world and from its historical future and, rather than being a continuation of this world, appeared to involve a radical break and discontinuity. Only occasionally in late texts do we hear in the Old Testament and in the intertestamental literature of a resurrection of the dead (Isa. 26:19; Dan. 12:2).

264. In contrast to the Old Testament the hope of the resurrection of the dead, a matter of dispute between Pharisees and Sadducees at the time of Jesus, is clearly attested in the *New Testament*. According to Paul it is inextricably linked to the resurrection of Jesus Christ himself, the first-born from the dead (1 Cor. 15:12ff.). We are born perishable but raised imperishable (1 Cor. 15:42; 53-54). Belief in the resurrection of the dead is a comfort for those who mourn the loss of friends (1 Thess. 4:13ff.). According to Acts, Paul's preaching of the resurrection of the dead in Athens was the subject which gave rise to special offence (Acts 17:32). In the Gospel of John this hope is linked to the certainty that the dead become alive at the voice of the Son of God (John 5:24ff.).

265. Eternal life is described in the New Testament as a personal existence with Christ (Phil. 1:23) but also portrayed as a fellowship in the kingdom of God united in the praise of the eternal God (Luke 13:29; Mark 14:25; Rev. 22:3; 7:12). The Old Testament figure of the new heaven and the new earth is adopted and taken further; we hear of the new city in which God will wipe away every tear from our eyes (Rev. 21:1ff.). Eternal life will be a life in the presence of God in which we shall see "face to face" (1 Cor. 13:12) what God is like (1 John 3:2). Fundamental to the New Testament witness is the fact that such life is not simply the object of hope but is also a present reality (cf. John's Gospel); the kingdom of God is already among us (Luke 17:21); new life is already given in baptism and we experience it as the fellowship of the Holy Spirit (Rom. 6:3 and 14:17). The gracious year of the Lord proclaimed by Isaiah as a promise for the future has already been fulfilled in the coming of Jesus (Luke 4:16-21).

II. Explication for today

266. To live by faith is to live in hope. The ground of our hope is Jesus Christ. As first-born from the dead, *Jesus Christ* is the realization and manifestation of the new humanity. In his life and work, death and resurrection, God manifests the future he intends for the world through the Spirit. In him, life eternal enters our lives, lifting them out of our bondage to death and bringing them into communion with God. The Spirit poured out by the Risen Christ is the seal of our hope which is a hope for what is beyond human capacities and expectations (Heb. 11:1), a hope against hope. But it is a confident hope because it rests on the powerful promise of God.

Resurrection of the dead

267. The focus and basis of our hope for life with God beyond death (1 Thess. 4:13-18; Matt. 25:31ff.; 1 Cor. 15:3ff.) is the resurrection of Jesus Christ from the dead and the promise that those who have died with Christ will live forever with him. For Christian faith resurrection means that human beings in their individuality and wholeness, body-soul-spirit, have a future beyond death and that therefore human existence from its beginning to the death of the individual has an eternal significance in accountability to God. This hope is a protest against the scepticism of those for whom death is the limit to all life. Transience and death are not the last word on human life, rather God has bestowed a unique dignity on human existence through promising eternal life. Resurrection implies for Christian faith that after death the human person has a future.

Commentary

The status of the dead between death and resurrection has been understood in various ways (e.g. in terms of purgatory after death). Different beliefs about the dead and their relation to the living led to different religious practices (e.g. prayers for the dead, intercession by the saints and invocation of the saints). Furthermore, the idea of the immortality of the soul, important for much of Christian history, has been both affirmed by some and denied by others in recent years.

268. Resurrection involves an encounter with the living God and his judgement of good and evil within personal and communal life. Humanity is accountable to him both now and at the final judgement. We believe and affirm that it is not the will of God to condemn and destroy the world

he has created. In giving his Son he wants his world to be saved (John 3:17). The biblical witness contains, however, the possibility of a final condemnation (e.g. Matt. 25:45f.; Rev. 20:15). The tension between these different emphases in the biblical witness should not be dissolved by rationalizing one way or another, but should be taken as indicating the openness of history.

Commentary

In the course of history, some Christian theologians and spiritual movements defended universal salvation. In the Bible, the phrase *apokatastasis panton* ("the time for establishing all") occurs in Acts 3:21, but relates to the final fulfilment of the Old Testament's prophecy and hardly implies universal salvation. Mark 9:12 says of Elijah that in the last days he will come again and "restore all things"; but in 9:13 Jesus interprets this as already realized in the ministry of John the Baptist. In 1 Tim. 2:4 it is said that God wants every human being to be saved and obtain the knowledge of his saving truth (cf. also Rom. 11:32). But while this provides a rationale for Christian mission, it does not include a guarantee of universal salvation for those who reject the call to conversion.

In faithfulness to the New Testament teaching, Christian doctrine has to do justice not only to the unlimited intention of God's saving love but also to the many New Testament warnings that eternal damnation is possible. Nevertheless the saving will of God remains an ultimate mystery which still keeps possibilities open where the record seems to be closed for human beings.

269. The death of human beings was regarded as the sharpest existential manifestion of the presence of powers of destruction everywhere in creation. These *forces of death* are present throughout life and seek to separate us from our brothers and sisters and from God. But death is conquered in the cross and resurrection of Christ which gives us assurance of our resurrection. In baptism (Rom. 6:3ff.) and throughout the Christian life, we participate in Christ's death, in his *victory over death* in his resurrection and receive his life-giving Spirit. At the same time Christ's death and resurrection and the coming of the Spirit point forward to the resurrection of the dead and to the final transformation of the cosmos.

The life of the world to come

270. According to God's purpose creation will be radically transformed in ways that are still a mystery. In Christ, God sets forth his "plan for the fullness of time, to unite all things in him, things in heaven and things on earth" (Eph. 1:10). Thus the wholeness of creation will not be separated from the final fulfilment of the kingdom of God. Some elements of creation like the water of baptism, human words proclaiming the gospel and the bread and the wine of the eucharist are already now used by the Holy Spirit to give us the first fruits of the kingdom. In the *new heaven and new earth* (Isa. 65:17; Rev. 21:1), the new humanity will see and praise God face to face (1 Cor. 13:12). God will be all in all (1 Cor. 15:28).

271. The kingdom is the fulfilment of the prophecy to Israel (Isa. 11:1-11; Micah 4:3) of the establishment of justice, righteousness and peace, God's will alone on earth as in heaven. The kingdom of God is the reality in which the sovereign reign of God is realized by the power of the Holy Spirit through his Son Jesus Christ. Under God's sovereign reign, the forces of evil, sin and death, the principalities and powers of the age (1 Cor. 15:22-24; Col. 2:15; etc.) are overcome through the cross and resurrection (Phil. 2:5-11).

Living in hope today

272. The Church is therefore a communion of hope within a world confronted by death and destruction. In the Church the reign of Christ is present in the world, where by the power of the Holy Spirit, reconciliation, peace, justice and renewal become realities already attainable. Thus, the Church is a sign of God's future for the renewal of humanity. The Church also looks forward to the final fulfilment. The Church's hope is thus a hope for the world and a trust in God's redemptive promise of faithfulness to his entire creation.

Commentary

For further detailed analysis see *Sharing in One Hope. Commission on Faith and Order, Bangalore 1978*; cf. *The Church: A Communion of Hope*, Part V of *A Common Account of Hope*, Faith and Order Paper No. 92, WCC, Geneva, 1978.

273. The Church has one hope: "You were called to the one hope that belongs to your call" (Eph. 4:4). This one hope brings together hope for the resurrection of the dead and the life of the world to come. These

belong inseparably together and affirm and undergird Christian hope in its social, individual and cosmic dimensions.

Living our hope

274. To believe in the life-giving and transforming power of the Holy Spirit; to be the koinonia of God's people in Christ's Church, sent to all people to proclaim and live the Good News of salvation until the end of history; to become through baptism for the forgiveness of sins partakers of the new life of the risen Lord; and to receive thereby the assurance of sharing with all creation in the life of the world to come — all these are constitutive elements of the apostolic faith throughout the ages. They give Christians today an unshakeable foundation and *new perspectives* for their involvement in the affairs of this world. This finds its central expression in our Christian hope in the midst of a threatened and finite world.

275. Filled with this hope and despite our own weakness and fears we can live with confidence and trust in the promises of God within a world that seems uncertain about its future. Because we believe that the future is in the sure hands of God, we need not be anxious for tomorrow (Matt. 6:34). We are impelled by our hope *to work for a more humane and just world*. Our pursuit of justice and peace within history cannot bring about the kingdom, but our work is done in the trust that nothing of what we have done in expectation of that Holy City will be in vain. Because our hope is grounded in God, we can risk opening ourselves to the joys and sufferings of the world.

276. Since by faith we affirm our hope for this world, a hope which is grounded in belief in the Triune God, we *reject any escape from this world* and its problems. Such escape may take many forms. We may, for example, lose ourselves in the accumulation of things, the pursuit of individual satisfaction or in an other-worldly flight away from the concrete needs of our neighbour.

— Affirming our trust in the future God has prepared for us, we reject any attempt to secure our future at the expense of the world, especially through the threat of either nuclear or ecological destruction.

— Affirming the presence of the yet future kingdom, we reject any understanding of God's coming kingdom which either separates the kingdom from this world and its life, or identifies the kingdom with any historical reality.

— Affirming God's faithfulness to his entire creation, we reject any impoverishment of our hope which blinds us to the wholeness of

God's redemption of individuals, of human community, or of all creation.

— Affirming that Jesus Christ with his Spirit is God's Word by which all is judged and its ultimate meaning is disclosed, we reject that the powers that seem to rule history will finally determine its meaning and destiny.

277. In the face of a purely secular outlook which does not extend beyond itself to God, *our hope* is active in love within this world while looking to the world to come, and is renewed within the communion of the Church through the ever new gift of God's salvation in Jesus Christ, given by the Holy Spirit through word and sacrament.

— In the face of despair over the world, our hope refuses to acquiesce in things as they are.

— In face of growing hopelessness, our hope will declare no situation or person beyond hope.

— In the face of oppression, our hope affirms that oppression will not remain forever.

— In the face of religious perspectives misused to justify political programmes, our hope affirms that the advent of the kingdom of God is not within our power, but remains in the power of God's surprising initiative.

— In the face of unbearable pain, incurable disease, and irreversible handicap, our hope affirms the loving presence of Christ who can make possible what is impossible to human powers.

270. Our hope for this life and this world is grounded in the cross and the resurrection of Jesus Christ, and it will find its consummation in the beatific vision and by participating in the joy of God in the communion of saints. *In God alone is our trust.* All that we have received, we have received from his hand. All that we hope for will come from his blessing. To God be glory from age to age. "He who testifies to these things, says, 'surely I am coming soon'. Amen. Come, Lord Jesus" (Rev. 22:30).

Amen

279. The Nicene-Constantinopolitan Creed ends with the *Amen*. Already in the Holy Scriptures this "Amen" is used to signify that the people of God receive and by this reception confirm a proclamation. In the early liturgies what had been proclaimed and confessed by the ministers in their specific office in the Church of God was so received and confirmed by the whole assembly, expressing its trust in what has been

confessed. Today when the whole assembly proclaims and confesses the Creed together with the ministers, it signifies the communion of the whole Church of God in the faith transmitted through the apostles. The Amen of this assembly confidently expresses the *yes* to the Triune God revealed to us as the Father, the Son and the Holy Spirit.

Historical Background of the Apostolic Faith Today

Gennadios Limouris

From 1888 to 1963

One of the first attempts in modern times to provide for the expression of the common faith was made in 1888 when the Third Lambeth Conference summarized thus the essentials of the Christian faith in the Lambeth Quadrilateral: "... the Apostles' Creed, as the baptismal symbol, and the Nicene Creed, as the sufficient statement of the Christian faith".[1]

Later, in 1910, upon the initiative of the Protestant Episcopal Church in the USA, the Faith and Order movement had its beginnings when an appeal was made to "all Christian Communions throughout the world which confess our Lord Jesus Christ as God and Saviour".[2]

Three events in 1920 marked further important steps in a long ecumenical process. In its Encyclical "Unto the Churches of Christ Everywhere" the Ecumenical Patriarchate of Constantinople urged the "creation of some form of a league of churches".[3] The Anglican bishops, assembled at the Lambeth Conference, issued an "Appeal to all Christian People" for the reunion of Christendom in which they addressed themselves to the question of faith.[4] Finally, the preparatory conference on Faith and Order, meeting in Geneva, Switzerland, in 1920, dealt with "the significance of the Bible and a Creed in relation to reunion".[5]

---

[1] See *The Five Lambeth Conferences 1867-1908, Lambeth Quadrilateral 1888*, Randall T. Davidson ed., London, SPCK, 1920.

[2] Faith and Order Series No. 1, 1910, p.4.

[3] Cf. C. Patelos ed., *The Orthodox Church in the Ecumenical Movement*, WCC, Geneva, 1978, pp.27-33.

[4] Henry Bettenson ed., *Documents of the Christian Church*, London, Oxford University Press, 2nd ed., 1963, pp.442ff.

[5] Cf. Especially the contribution by A. Scott and J.E. Roberts, in the report of the preliminary meeting in Geneva, Switzerland (12-20 August 1920), *A Pilgrimage Towards Unity*, in: Faith and Order Series No. 33, 1920, pp.54,72.

The agenda of the first world conference on Faith and Order in Lausanne, Switzerland, in 1927 already included a section on "The Church's Common Confession of Faith".[6]

At the second world conference on Faith and Order, in Edinburgh, Scotland, in 1937, the substantial findings on the question of the common faith were put together in the report on "The Grace of Our Lord Jesus Christ".[7]

After the formation of the World Council of Churches and its first assembly in Amsterdam, Holland, in 1948, the main concern for the third world conference on Faith and Order, held in Lund, Sweden, in 1952, was to ensure that the faith in the one Church of Christ be translated into acts of obedience.[8]

The fourth world conference, meeting in Montreal, Canada, in 1963, affirmed that the understanding of the Christian faith was inter-related with questions of "Scripture, Tradition and traditions".[9]

From 1963 to 1983

Since Montreal, the Faith and Order Commission has steadily continued to pursue the question of the common understanding and confession of the one Christian faith. This became apparent above all in the study on "Giving Account of the Hope that is in Us" which was initiated at the Louvain (Belgium) Commission meeting in 1971 and concluded at the Bangalore (India) Commission meeting in 1978 where the statement "A Common Account of the Hope" dealt with the Trinitarian faith in God, ecclesiology, eschatology and ethics and the requirement for a consensus on the apostolic faith.[10]

At the Lima (Peru) Commission meeting in 1982, a plan was outlined for a new study project "Towards the Common Expression of the Apostolic Faith Today", emphasizing the importance of the theme in general and of the Nicene Creed in particular for the ecumenical movement of today.[11]

---

[6] L. Vischer ed., *A Documentary History of the Faith and Order Movement 1927-1963*, St Louis, Missouri, Bethany Press, 1963, pp.27,29,31.

[7] *Ibid.*, pp.40ff.

[8] *Ibid.*, p.86.

[9] P.C. Rodger & L. Vischer eds., *The Fourth World Conference on Faith and Order, Montreal 1963*, Faith and Order Paper No. 42, SCM Press, London, 1964, Section II: "Scripture, Tradition, traditions", pp.50-61.

[10] Cf. *Sharing in One Hope, Bangalore 1978*, "The Common Expression of the Apostolic Faith", Faith and Order Paper No. 92, WCC, Geneva, 1978, pp.243-246.

[11] M. Kinnamon ed., *Towards Visible Unity II, Lima 1982*, Faith and Order Paper No. 113, WCC, Geneva, 1982, pp.28-46.

But this new beginning had already been prepared through smaller consultations on "Towards a Confession of the Common Faith" in Venice, Italy, in 1978[12] and on the *Filioque* question in Klingenthal, France, in 1978/79,[13] and in relation to the 1600th anniversary of the Second Ecumenical Council. At these consultations the Nicene-Constantinopolitan Creed (381) was chosen to be the focus from which further studies would be pursued during the forthcoming years in order to explicate the apostolic faith, as it is expressed and confessed in the Church through this credal symbol of unity in the early Church. This decision was taken at a small consultation in Chambésy, Switzerland, in 1981,[14] and later the same year at another consultation in Odessa, USSR, first steps were undertaken.[15] Both meetings reflected the ecumenical significance of the Nicene-Constantinopolitan Creed of 381. And, in Rome in 1983, an international consultation focused on the roots of the apostolic faith in the forms in which it was expressed in the Scriptures of the Old and New Testaments and in the early Church.[16]

In Vancouver (Canada) in 1983, the sixth assembly of the World Council of Churches strongly affirmed the significance and importance of this study[17] and since 1984 it was steadily implemented. A series of booklets with contemporary expressions of the faith in different countries[18] and a documentary collection of texts[19] have accompanied the study.

---

[12] *Towards a Confession of the Common Faith,* Faith and Order Paper No. 100, WCC, Geneva, 1980.

[13] L. Vischer ed., *Spirit of God — Spirit of Christ. Ecumenical Reflections on the Filioque Controversy,* Faith and Order Paper No. 103, WCC, Geneva, 1981.

[14] *Towards the Common Expression of the Apostolic Faith,* FO/81:9 (August 1981), mimeographed paper.

[15] *The Ecumenical Importance of the Nicene-Constantinopolitan Creed,* FO/81:17 (November 1981), mimeographed paper.

[16] H.-G. Link ed., *The Roots of Our Common Faith: Faith in the Scriptures and in the Early Church,* Faith and Order Paper No. 119, WCC, Geneva, 1984.

[17] D. Gill ed., *Gathered for Life,* Official Report of the Sixth Assembly, Vancouver/Canada (1983), WCC, Geneva, 1983, p.48.

[18] *Confessing Our Faith Around the World I,* C.S. Song ed., Faith and Order Paper No. 104, WCC, Geneva, 1980; *Confessing Our Faith Around the World II,* H.-G. Link ed., Faith and Order Paper No. 120, WCC, Geneva, 1983; *Confessing Our Faith Around the World III: the Caribbean and Central America,* H.-G. Link ed., Faith and Order Paper No. 123, WCC, Geneva, 1984; *Confessing Our Faith Around the World IV: South America,* H.-G. Link ed., Faith and Order Paper No. 126, WCC, Geneva, 1985.

[19] H.-G. Link ed., *Apostolic Faith Today. A Handbook for Study,* Faith and Order Paper No. 124, WCC, Geneva, 1985.

From 1984 to 1986

At its first meeting in Crete, Greece, in 1984, the new Faith and Order Standing Commission decided to attempt a comprehensive ecumenical explication of the apostolic faith for our time, taking into consideration the decisions and preliminary discussions of 1981 and 1983, and to take up the Nicene-Constantinopolitan Creed of 381 as the most striking model of unity in the early Church for the new beginning of the study.[20] An Apostolic Faith Steering Group was established, composed of members of the Standing Commission, with the task to coordinate, together with the Geneva Secretariat and the full Commission, the process of study and to inform the Commission regularly about the progress made. Three international consultations were held, each considering one article of the Creed:

— Kottayam, India, November 1984: *We believe in one Lord Jesus Christ* (second article)
— Chantilly, France, January 1985: *We believe in the Holy Spirit, the Church and the Life of the World to Come* (third article)
— Kinshasa, Zaire, March 1985: *We believe in the one God* (first article).

As a second step, a small drafting group met in April 1985 in Geneva, and the Steering Group of the Apostolic Faith study came together in May/June 1985, at Crêt-Bérard, Switzerland, in order to revise and further develop the format of the reports of the three consultations and submit them to the Plenary Commission meeting in Stavanger, Norway, in August 1985.[21]

In May 1986, a joint consultation between the sub-units of "Faith and Order" and "Church and Society" took place in York, England, on the theme "Integrity of Creation" for a first exchange of the programmatic emphases in the two sub-units, as part of Faith and Order's study project on the Apostolic Faith.[22]

On the basis of the Stavanger proposals, a revised preliminary draft text, elaborated by the staff in March/April 1986, the Steering Group of

---

[20] *Minutes of the Meeting of the Standing Commission, Crete 1984,* Faith and Order Paper No. 121, WCC, Geneva, 1984, pp.11-19.
[21] Thomas F. Best ed., *Faith and Renewal, Stavanger 1985,* Faith and Order Paper No. 131, WCC, Geneva, 1986, pp.127-143.
[22] *Minutes of the Meeting of the Standing Commission, Potsdam, GDR, 1986,* Faith and Order Paper No. 134, WCC, Geneva, 1986, pp.25-27.

the Apostolic Faith study met again in West Berlin, FRG, in July 1986, with the task to review, correct and share the text on the ecumenical explication with the Standing Commission in Potsdam, GDR. [23]

From 1987 to 1990

The Steering Group met again in Paris, France, in April 1987, in order to finalize the draft text on the "explication" and to incorporate comments and suggestions made by Standing Commission members.

The Standing Commission, at its meeting in Madrid, Spain, in August 1987, approved the study document *Confessing One Faith*[24] in its provisional form and authorized its publication which was done in October of the same year. It was sent to the member churches and the wider ecumenical community for study and comments.

The period 1987-1990 has been marked by a considerable number of reactions, comments and suggestions sent to the Geneva Secretariat from theologians, ecumenical institutes, theological faculties, study groups, and Faith and Order Commission members around the world. Parallel to this, a second series of international consultations — in relation to the study document *Confessing One Faith* — took place in different parts of the world, with participants from various Christian traditions, who reacted either directly to the text itself or provided suggestions and perspectives regarding the text on issues related to the contemporary world situation and to theological conversations in particular:

— Porto Alegre, Brazil, November 1987: *The Doctrine of Creation and Its Integrity — A Challenge to the Responsibility of Christianity Today*[25]
— Rhodes, Greece, January 1988: *Confessing the Crucified and Risen Christ in the Social, Cultural and Ethical Context of Today*[26]
— Dublin (Ireland), May 1988: *Creation and the Kingdom of God*; this second joint consultation of the sub-units on Faith and Order and Church and Society focused on and explored questions of the integrity

---

[23] *Ibid.*, pp.41-42.
[24] *Confessing One Faith*, Faith and Order Paper No. 140, WCC, Geneva, 1987.
[25] *The Doctrine of Creation and Its Integrity — A Challenge to the Responsibility of Christianity Today, Minutes of the Meeting of the Standing Commission 1988*, Faith and Order Paper No. 145, WCC, Geneva, 1988, pp.45ff.
[26] *Confessing the Crucified and Risen Christ in the Social, Cultural and Ethical Context of Today, Minutes of the Meeting of the Standing Commission 1988*, Faith and Order Paper No. 145, WCC, Geneva, 1988, pp.56ff.

of creation in light of challenging global issues in the context of the theology of creation and from the insights of Church and Society programmes[27]

— Pyatigorsk, USSR, November 1988: *Ecclesiology — Basic Ecumenical Perspectives* (where ecclesiology was seen as common to the three main study projects of the Faith and Order Commission: (i) BEM process, (ii) Apostolic Faith, and (iii) Unity and Renewal[28]

— Würzburg, FRG, June 1989: *Ecumenical Reflections on the Holy Spirit in Creation, Church and History,*[29] also related to the main theme of the seventh assembly of the WCC in Canberra, Australia, February 1991, *"Come, Holy Spirit — Renew the Whole Creation*[30]

In September 1988, the Faith and Order Standing Commission, meeting in Boston (USA), was informed about the process of revision by the Steering Group (which had met briefly after the Rhodes consultation) and it endorsed the results achieved and the efforts undertaken at the three international consultations.[31]

Meanwhile the Steering Group on the Apostolic Faith study met in Rome, Italy, in March/April 1989, in order to attempt a first evaluation of the suggestions and comments sent to the Geneva Secretariat on the study document *Confessing One Faith*.

The Plenary Commission, meeting in Budapest, Hungary, in August 1989, heard reports on the ongoing process of revision and made detailed plans for the next steps to be undertaken.[32]

The year 1990 was then devoted entirely to meetings of the Apostolic Faith Steering Group in order to finalize the revision of the three sections of the study document. In January 1990, at the meeting in Oxford, England, the first article was considerably revised and, at the meeting in Venice, Italy, in April 1990, the second and third articles were substantially revised.

---

[27] *Creation and the Kingdom of God*, D. Gosling & G. Limouris eds, *Church and Society Documents*, No. 5 (August 1988).

[28] *Ecclesiology — Basic Ecumenical Perspectives*, FO/89:1 (January 1989), mimeographed paper.

[29] *Ecumenical Reflections on the Holy Spirit in Creation, Church and History*, FO/89:13A (October 1989), mimeographed paper.

[30] *Come, Holy Spirit — Renew the Whole Creation, Resources for Sections — The Theme, Sub-themes and Issues*, WCC seventh assembly 1991, WCC, Geneva, 1990 (mimeographed brochure).

[31] Cf. *Minutes of the Standing Commission 1988, op.cit.*, pp.45-53, 56-63 and FO/89:1 (mimeographed paper).

[32] *Faith and Order 1985-1989. The Commission Meeting at Budapest 1989*, Thomas F. Best ed., Faith and Order Paper No. 148, WCC, Geneva, 1990.

Finally, at its meeting in Dunblane, Scotland, in August 1990, the Standing Commission approved the revised version and authorized the official publication of the document in its new revised version under the title *Confessing the One Faith*. The publication will be sent to the churches for study and further consideration, accompanied by a letter from the Standing Commission, in order to facilitate the work for the churches to better understand and study the text within the context of their ecumenical encounters. In order to broaden involvement in the study of the apostolic faith, the Standing Commission also authorized the preparation of a (short) "Study Instrument" to be completed by 1992.

The document *Confessing the One Faith* will play a considerable role also at the forthcoming fifth world conference on Faith and Order, scheduled for 1993.

In the nearly ten years of the study process on the apostolic faith many have participated in various capacities, from different churches and traditions, contributing their Christian witness and experience to the process of explicating the apostolic faith in the ecumenical situation of today. Their contributions are much appreciated, and if the provisional goal set by the study has been reached, this is also due to their deep ecumenical commitment to the unity of the Church.

APPENDIX II

Glossary

Gennadios Limouris

Abba: An Aramaic Hebrew word meaning "father" and signifying deep intimacy in child-father relationships. It was used by Jesus Christ in his relationship with and prayer to God and became a cause of offence to and controversy with the Jewish religious authorities of his time (cf. Mark 14:36). The early Christians as followers of Christ, united with him through the Spirit, also used the term (cf. Rom. 8:15 and Gal. 4:6).

Almighty: The Greek equivalent of this term, *Pantokrator*, which is found in the original Greek text of the Nicene Creed and is used in the New Testament, adopted from the Greek Old Testament (the Septuagint, LXX), denotes God's power in upholding and sustaining all things. The Hebrew original "Lord Almighty" = *Adonai Sabaoth* means that God continues to uphold with his powers ("energies") all creation. Similar to this is also the meaning of the term "omnipotent". In neither case should the understanding of the terms be associated with the notion of domination.

Amen: The term has Hebrew origins and was adopted by Christians in every context and language. It derives from a Hebrew root meaning "truth"; hence its meaning: *truly*, indeed. It is usually used in liturgical literature, at the end of hymns or prayers, and denotes not only affirmation but also a wish: "truly" and "let it be so".

Apokatastasis: The phrase has biblical roots (cf. Mal. 3:23 (LXX); Mark 9:12; Matt. 17:11; Acts 1:6; 3:21). The Greek word meaning "restoration" was adopted as a technical term in the discussion of the Christian doctrine of salvation and especially of the "last things" (cf. Acts 3:21). It is also connected with the theory of "the final restoration of all things", *apokatastasis panton*, also signifying "universalism", in particular in Origen's thought. Origen's use of the phrase gave it theological importance. Views of salvation were in real tension. Not only was there tension between individualistic and universalistic views, but also between salvation conceived as a radical change for the better, totally discontinuous with the accidents of the present life, and salvation conceived as a process guided by God's providence which takes souls upwards towards participation in the divine life itself. Origen's genius was to attempt to incorporate the two perspectives by affirming both that the present conditions of existence are to be removed and that the life of the soul establishes continuity in history. However, Origen's doctrine was condemned as heresy by the early Church.

Apostolic succession: A technical term denoting the historical continuity in *Holy Orders* (primarily episcopal, but also presbyteral) going back to the apostles. It is intimately connected with the more comprehensive "apostolic tradition", the historical continuity in faith, life and mission since the period of the apostles. The concept also underlies much controversy among the churches of the West, in particular since the Reformation, and remains a principal obstacle to the mutual recognition of ministries in the divided Church.

In the course of the ecumenical movement theologians returned to the recognition that apostolic succession is primarily manifested in the apostolic tradition of the Church as a whole, whereas the apostolic succession of the ministry exists to serve that of which it is itself a sign.

Apostolicity: "Apostolicity" is referred to as one of the marks of the Church mentioned in the Nicene Creed; it is founded on the apostles and is in continuity with them (Eph. 2:19ff.). It was used in this sense by a number of early Christian writers, and in particular by Tertullian and Augustine as a criterion of orthodoxy, but it was the sixteenth century Reformation that gave it a particular significance, the Roman Catholics focusing on the apostolic succession of the episcopacy and the Reformation churches on the primitive and therefore pure form of Christianity.

Apostolicity, in the sense of faithfulness to the witness of the apostles, is a mark of the Church, and therefore it is expressed in the whole life of the Church, not just in its organizational structure.

Begotten not made: This phrase is found in the second article of the Creed and it was used to distinguish the Logos/Son of God who became incarnate and appeared as "Jesus Christ our Lord" from all created beings angelic or human. In the early centuries before the First Ecumenical Council of Nicea (325) such a distinction had not been clearly articulated, although the thought was upheld by the theologians of the Church. The fourth-century heresy of Arianism which denied that Jesus Christ was truly God as Son and Word of God led the Church to define this clear distinction and affirm Christ's true Godhead.

Catholicity: According to its original Greek root *(katholikotes)* this word means totality as *distinct from partiality.* It denotes the whole, or wholeness, as opposed to a part or parts. When applied to spiritual entities, it also signifies integrity and perfection. When associated with the Church, it retains the notion of wholeness and integrity but is extended to the notion of universality or ecumenicity. Thus the catholicity of the Church implies not only the integrity of the local churches in a universal communion *(koinonia)* but also their inner unity and cohesion due to this integrity.

Charism: This term is based on the Greek New Testament term *charisma* which denotes "a gift" of the Holy Spirit granted to Christians for the upbuilding of the community (cf. Rom. 11:29, 12:6; 1 Cor. 1:7, 12:4, 9, 28, 30, 31; 1 Tim. 4:14, 1:6; 1 Pet. 4:10).

Christos-Kyrios: The association of the two names "Christ" and "Lord" (Luke 2:11) and of both with the name of "Jesus" is very common in the New Testament. It conveys the belief of the early Christians in the absolute and divine authority of Jesus Christ and implies his unique divine-human status.

Communion (koinonia): This term is rich in content and associations. It is used in connection with the Holy Trinity, and the relationship of Christians with God and one another *in*, *through* and *with* Christ and the Holy Spirit. It basically means "sharing together", "participating in" or "having in common". In the case of the Trinity, communion means that the Father, the Son and the Holy Spirit always exist and act together in a communion of love, though they are distinct. The three persons have in common all that the Father has given to the Son and all that the Spirit possesses as well by virtue of being the Spirit of the Father who always abides in the Son. Christian communion is a real reflection on the human level of the Divine Communion, based on the union of the divine and human realities in Christ (1 Cor. 1:9; 1 John 1:3, 6, 7). Its source is the communion with the living Christ through his Word and sacrament, particularly in the eucharist which is fittingly called "holy communion" (1 Cor. 10:16; cf. Acts 2:42). Crucial here is the role of the Holy Spirit in profoundly influencing the whole reality of human life. Hence the New Testament speaks of "the communion of the Holy Spirit" (2 Cor. 13:13; Phil. 2:1).

Consubstantial: This is the English term traditionally used for translating the crucial Greek term *homoousios* (from *homos* = together and *ousia* = substance, being, existence) of the Nicene Creed. It means that the Son or Word of God not only is from the Father but is actually "one in (substance) being" or co-existing (consubstantial) with the Father from all eternity. Not only did the Son not come into being out of nothing (or non-being) but, actually, there was not any duration of time or eternity when he was not. Thus the term "consubstantial" stands for the real and eternal unity in being or existence of the Son with the Father.

The term "consubstantial" is not used today as extensively as in the past because "substance" no longer conveys what it did in the past; it is often replaced by the terms "one in being" or "co-existing".

Covenant: "Covenant" or "Testament" (*berith* in Hebrew and *diathéke* in Greek) stands for the design or plan given by God for his relationship with his people. The Giver of the Covenant is God the Father but the actual giving is accomplished through God's Word (Son) and in God's Spirit, though human agents are also involved. There are two basic Covenants (cf. Rom. 9:4; Gal. 4:24; Eph. 2:12; 2 Cor. 2:14): the old one which was given to the people of Israel and whose supreme agent or mediator was Moses (cf. Ex. 3:7-10, 16; 14:31), and the new one, which extended and fulfilled the old one so as to include all peoples and nations and whose unique agent/mediator is the Lord Jesus Christ (cf. Heb. 8:6, 9:15, 12:24). Besides the Covenant with Israel, inaugurated through Moses, the Old Testament speaks also of a Covenant with Abraham (cf. Gen. 12:7; 13:15; 15:18) in which the promise of possession of the land of Canaan by his progeny plays a central part. The earlier Covenant with Noah (Gen. 9) was "with every living creature".

In the new universal Covenant God's Word is incarnate and identical with Jesus Christ, ratified in the shedding of his blood (cf. Luke 22:20; Matt. 26:28; Mark 14:24; Heb. 9:20, 10:29, 13:20), and the spirit of God's promises abides in him and is given through him (cf. Acts 2:33; Gal. 3:14, 22; Eph. 1:13, 3:1-12, etc.).

Creator Spiritus: This Latin form of the phrase "Creator Spirit" is often used by theologians to stress the involvement or the role of the Holy Spirit in creation and especially in creating life (cf. Gen. 1:2; John 6:63; Rom. 8:11; 1 Cor. 15:45).

Diakonia: The Greek New Testament term for "ministry" or "service", which has a wide range of applications within Christian life, characterizing all of it and particular aspects of it. Christ himself came as a *diakonos* (= deacon), a "servant", a "minister" who serves (Matt. 20:25) and asked every disciple of his to be "a servant for all" (Mark 9:35). St Paul extensively employed this term and in one instance he spoke of the "divisions" (different kinds) of diakonia (cf. 1 Cor. 12:5).

Divine Being: By Divine Being or God's Being we mean who God is. Jewish and Christian theologians are unanimous about the incomprehensibility and indeed unknowability of God's Being, i.e. what God is. Statements like "God is Light", Spirit, good, love, etc. refer to God's being, but they are not identical with it. None of these names or attributes traditionally applied to God can grasp fully or define adequately the Divine Being.

The great Jewish writer Philo of Alexandria (first century), who influenced many of the early Church Fathers, expressed this point very aptly when he said that God is "anonymous" (has no name) with respect to his Being but *polyonymous* (has many names) with respect to his attributes which are related to his acts or energies. There is a Christian theological tradition emanating from the medieval West which identifies God's attributes with his Divine Being. Yet even this tradition maintains that ultimately God's Being is like an unfathomable ocean. Even the affirmation of the unity of the Divine Being is a mystery which cannot be defined by either numerical or generic categories of human rationality.

Economy: The Greek term "economy" (in Greek *oikonomia*) originally used by St Paul (cf. 1 Cor. 9:17; Eph. 1:10, 3:2, 9; Col. 1:25 and 1 Tim. 1:4) denotes the whole plan of salvation revealed and worked out by God in Jesus Christ. The term was extensively employed by the early Church theologians and came to mean the incarnation of the Son of God and all its far-reaching consequences for the salvation of humankind and the restoration of order *(nomos)* in God's creation *(oikos)*. As such it was distinguished from the term *theologia* which referred to God's unity of Being in the Trinity of Father, Son and Spirit.

Epiklesis: A Greek term meaning "invocation", which is always connected with Christian prayer to God for the gift of the Holy Spirit. Its primary context, especially for Eastern Orthodox Christians, is the celebration of the eucharist and the actual consecration of the eucharistic gifts of the Body and Blood of Christ for the common spiritual benefit of the participants, and this petition is located after the *anamnesis* (words of institution).

In the Egyptian *anaphora* of Serapion there was a petition before the institution account for the Son and Spirit to enlighten and strengthen the Church in proclaiming the gospel, and a petition after the institution account for the *Logos* to come upon the elements and bless the assembled participants.

In the Roman *anaphora* before the institution account there was a petition for consecration directed to the Father, and another after the *anamnesis*, asking for the favourable acceptance of the entire sacrifice by the Father so that its spiritual benefits might be shared by the participants: in neither petition was the Holy Spirit mentioned. Recent Roman reforms have added a pneumatic *epiklesis* before and after the institution narrative according to the Egyptian structure.

Eschatology — eschatological: A Greek term denoting whatever relates to the *eschaton* or *eschata* meaning the "final things" connected with the "end" (in Greek *telos*) of humankind and the world, which are brought about through God's action in and through Christ. In the New Testament Christ is called "the last Adam" (*eschatos Adam*, 1 Cor. 15:45), or "the first and the last" (cf. Rev. 1:11, 17, 2:18, 22:13) inasmuch as he has fulfilled in himself through his death and resurrection God's ultimate design for humankind and the world. The period which extends from his ascension to his second coming is eschatological because it is governed by the Risen Christ who is its ultimate *(eschatos)* destiny.

Ex nihilo: A Latin term meaning "out of nothing". In Christian theology it refers to the creation of the world and all that belongs to it. It is God who brings everything into being out of non-being (cf. 2 Macc. 7:28; Ps. 32:9; Heb. 11:3; Rom. 4:17).

Filioque: A Latin term meaning "and from the Son" which was added to the third article of the Nicene Creed in the Latin West. This addition became one of the causes of controversy and division between Western and Eastern churches from the ninth century to the present time. Its introduction into the Creed was understood by the East as changing the original doctrine of the single procession of the Holy Spirit from the Father (taken from John 15:26) into a doctrine of "double procession" which affected the traditional doctrine of the Trinity. In contemporary theological discussions between Roman Catholic, Protestant and Orthodox Christians many of the issues involved in the dispute over the "Filioque" have been clarified. Nevertheless the problem has not yet been officially solved, even though some of the upholders of the "Filioque" addition to the Creed are prepared "to remove" the addition on certain "ecumenical" occasions or even permanently. The Old Catholics have removed the addition from the liturgical recitation of the Creed, but do not necessarily find it incorrect (i.e. it can be interpreted in a correct way theologically, but was a one-sided addition to the Creed).

Sixteen centuries have passed since the Ecumenical Council of Constantinople (381) in which the Nicene-Constantinopolitan Creed originated. Received by the Church as the expression of the common apostolic faith, it has tragically also become a source of disagreement and disunity.

For an overview of recent discussions in ecumenical perspective, see *Spirit of God — Spirit of Christ. Ecumenical Reflections on the "Filioque" Controversy*, L. Vischer (ed.), Faith and Order Paper No. 103, SPCK/WCC, London/Geneva, 1981.

Homologoumen: A Greek word meaning "we confess" which comes from the verb *homologo* = confess (lit. "I repeat the same words" or "I uphold the same faith"). Both in the New Testament and in the Christian tradition it denotes an essential act on the part of the Christians within the Church.

Homoousios: See "consubstantial".

Hypostasis: See "person".

Immanence-transcendence: These two terms have been applied in Christian theology to the theme of God's relation to the world in order to denote respectively his presence in the world and his being "beyond" the world. In the traditional theology of the Fathers of the Church "immanence" is connected with God's acts in creation and redemption, while "transcendence" refers to God's being (cf. "Divine Being" in this glossary). It is important for Christians to uphold *both* God's immanence and transcendence, because to separate them would mean to fall into the two kinds of heresy, pantheism (which sees God entirely immanent in everything in the world) and dualism, Gnostic or Deist (which separates God from creation). The former error leads to idolatry and the latter to transcendental spiritualism or atheistic secularism.

Katholiké: A Greek word *kath'olon* (meaning "catholic" in English) and used in the Nicene Creed as one of the four essential marks of the Church (cf. "Catholicity" in this glossary).

Kenosis = emptiness: An important Greek theological term meaning "emptying" or emptiness. It is derived from the pivotal Pauline statement about Christ in Phil. 2:7, according to which "Jesus Christ, though he was in the form of God ... emptied *(ekénosen)* himself, taking the form of a servant, being born in the likeness of human beings ...". It was employed by many of the early Church Fathers, especially by St Cyril of Alexandria, in their exposition of the incarnation. Kenotic love is taken as constitutive of God's being. Expressed through reciprocal divine-human self-giving in Christ, God's love overcomes evil and creates salvation through death and resurrection. Theories of *kenosis*, arising in sixteenth-century debate, were revived in the nineteenth century to re-interpret classical doctrines of incarnation. They have been explored again, notably by Barth and Rahner.

Koinonia: See "communion".

"Leitourgia" — *liturgy:* A Greek term often used as "liturgy" or "service". It is specifically used with reference to worship and the celebration of the eucharist (holy communion). In its original Greek form it means "function" *(érgon)* of the people *(laos)*. In the Christian context it refers both to the eucharistic function of the local church and to its social implications in the Christian community. In the New Testament, Christ, the apostles, Christian leaders and the faithful are all called liturgists *(leitourgoi)* whose liturgies are distinct but certainly inter-related and coordinated. Closely connected, even identified with this term, is the term "diakonia" (see this glossary) as referred to, for instance, in 2 Cor. 9:12.

Local (universal) church: See "catholicity".

Logos: One of the most famous and meaningful Greek words meaning "Word" and applied in the prologue to St John's Gospel to Jesus Christ, God's Son (cf. John 1:1). No other term has been so extensively used in the early Church and subsequently in classical Patristic theology, in the discussion of Christology and pneumatology. Jesus Christ has been understood in classical Christian theology as the eternal Logos (Word) of God (John 1:1) who became flesh (John 1:14) for the salvation of humankind. Christian theology has spoken also of the Logos of God in God, in creation, in human being and in redemption.

Messiahship: This word is based on the Hebrew word *Messiah* meaning "the anointed One" (of God) — *Christos* — whose coming is the great expectation of the Jewish people. The origins of the word are to be found in the Old Testament in the idea of anointing persons for particular tasks (cf. 1 Sam. 24:6; Lev. 4:3ff.; Isa. 45:1; 61:1; 1 Kings 19:16; Ps. 89:38). In the New Testament the term has been used to elucidate the Christian understanding of Jesus' identity and mission (Mark 8:29; Acts 2:36). The Christian meaning of the term goes beyond the Hebrew one in affirming that Jesus is the Messiah not only as "the anointed" but also as "the anointing one". As St Athanasius of Alexandria expressed it, "He as God anoints himself as man so that his human anointing might pass to all human beings".

Messianic belief was one facet of the eschatological beliefs of Judaism. The future hope lies in its essential outlines, but the place and prominence of the Messiah in these hopes varied greatly. Two constant elements in the eschatological hope were the expectation that there would be a period of tribulation before the coming of the new age and the expectation that God's reign would be established on earth. Not every text gives prominence to the Messiah in this process.

Millenarianism: From *millennium* which means "a thousand years". The term denotes those people in the early Church who literally believed that Christ would come again and reign on earth only for a thousand years! This view has been revived in the course of church history (cf. for example Joachim of Fiore) and also today among some groups including Jehovah's Witnesses.

Mystery ("mysterion"): The New Testament understanding of this word can be rendered by the expression "open secret". It denotes a truth which is revealed but escapes total comprehension. Such truths are God's Being (revealed through his acts); Jesus Christ the Word/Son of God, who became man without ceasing to be God; the salvation achieved by Christ and experienced by Christians; the Church's identity, as both divine and human.

For further description and development of the theme "mystery" in relation to ecclesiology, see *Church — Kingdom — World. The Church as Mystery and Sign,* G. Limouris ed., Faith and Order Paper No. 130, WCC, Geneva, 1986.

Pantokrator: See "Almighty".

Person ("Hypostasis"): This term in its original Latin form *persona* (and *prosopon* in Greek) was applied in the early centuries to the Father, or/and the Son, or/and the Holy Spirit. By the first Christian century it was in normal use and meant simply an individual human being. *Persona* was the natural Latin equivalent of the Greek *prosopon* which itself could carry the meaning of "human individual", but whose most persistent connotation was that of "face" or "countenance". *Persona* was introduced into the theological vocabulary in consequence of its use to render *prosopon*.

It was Tertullian who gave the word "person" its technical status in Trinitarian and Christological discourse. He affirmed that in the Christian perception of God there was an arrangement (dispensation) of three persons, and to fail to admit that meant to fall into the error of "monarchianism" and, in effect, deny the revelation of God in Christ. Monarchianism denied the trinity of persons and identified Father, Son and Holy Spirit as *one God* and *one Person.* It took two forms, which are known as dynamic monarchianism, represented by Paul of Samosata, and modalistic monarchianism, represented by the great "systematizer" — the heretic Sabellius. By the end of the fourth century and after the condemnation of Arianism it had been universally accepted among the Orthodox that, in the Christian conception of God there is one essence (*ousia,* substance, being) in three persons (*hypostasis).* Thus, through the clarifications of these terms, Christians affirmed both the unity and the Trinity of God. Contemporary theologians are faced with the problem of clarifying these terms once again because they have come to mean different things in contemporary secular usage.

Ru'ah (Spirit): The Hebrew term for the word Spirit — especially the Spirit of God.

Shechinah: A Hebrew word denoting the "mercy seat" in the holy of holies of the Jewish sanctuary where the glory (*Kabodh* in Hebrew) of God rested and was revealed. In the Christian Church it has been replaced by the presence of Christ and finds its best expression in the life of the Church in Word and sacrament (cf. Ex. 25:17; Rom. 3:25; Heb. 9:5ff.).

Soteriology — soteriological: A Greek word *soteria* denoting what pertains or relates to salvation. It also qualifies whatever has saving significance.

Spirituality: A term which is frequently used today in ecumenical debates and which refers to the patterns of Christian life, worship, prayer, piety. It is also especially applicable to the various life-patterns of the ascetics. Generally it relates to "the life of the Spirit" or "life in Christ".

Theodicy: Greek term meaning "putting God to trial". A classic biblical case of a theodicy is found in the story of Job. Generally the term refers to the question why evil and suffering exist in the world despite a good and loving God.

Theos-Kyrios: Two Greek terms often appearing together in the Holy Scriptures to denote "God-the-Lord" or the "Lord-God".

Theotokos (Mother of God, Virgin Mary): A Greek term meaning "Bearer of God" or "Mother of God" applied to the Virgin Mary. It was extensively used in the early Church from the second century onwards but became a cause of controversy in the beginning of the fifth century. Nestorius of Constantinople argued in 428/429 that the Virgin Mary could not be called "Theotokos" because she gave birth only to the man Jesus and not to the Son/Logos of God who was eternally begotten from the very being of the Father according to the original text of the Nicene Creed (325). St Cyril of Alexandria argued that, contrary to Nestorius' explanation, one had to apply this term to the Virgin Mary who did not bear a mere man (Jesus) but the eternal Son of God who become also a man by assuming individual human nature from his Virgin Mother.

The Third Ecumenical Council of Ephesus (431-433) condemned Nestorius and his position and made the term "Theotokos" a mark of Orthodox Christology alongside the Nicene term *homoousios*. The same doctrine was ratified by the Fourth (451), Fifth (553), Sixth (680-681) and Seventh (787) Ecumenical Councils. Excessive veneration of the Virgin Mary and the rise of Latin medieval Mariology led some of the Reformers and their successors to adopt a critical or differentiated position concerning Mariology. Modern ecumenical discussions are helping to clarify the old issues and move towards a balanced understanding and appreciation of the term "Theotokos".

Torah: The Hebrew word for "law", usually referring primarily to the Pentateuch, the first five books of the Old Testament, but also to the entire Jewish religious tradition.

Typos: A Greek word meaning "model" or even "prototype".

Virginity (of Mary): That Jesus Christ was born of the Virgin Mary is the witness of Matthew and Luke and of all the Church writers in the Early Church and of the Nicene Creed. From the beginning of the Christian era the virginity was understood by the theologians of the early Church as bearing witness to the Divine Person of Christ and to his truly becoming human without ceasing to be divine. It was also linked with the fact that Christ was the second Adam (Paul) inasmuch as he too, like the first Adam, did not have a human father (notably affirmed by St Irenaeus of Lyons).

Bibliography

Gennadios Limouris

This short bibliography refers either to Faith and Order publications on the Apostolic Faith study or to subjects which are related to it. Titles are given in order of publication. We apologize for being so selective and for any omission.

For further bibliographical references see *Dictionary of the Ecumenical Movement*, N. Lossky, J. Míguez Bonino, J.S. Pobee, T.F. Stransky, G. Wainwright & P. Webb (eds.), WCC/Geneva and Eerdmans/Grand Rapids, 1991 (editor's note).

Towards a Confession of the Common Faith, P. Duprey and L. Vischer (eds.), Faith and Order Paper No. 100, WCC, Geneva, 1980.

Vers une profession de foi commune, Document de Foi et constitution no. 100, COE, Genève, 1980.

"Auf dem Weg zu einem Bekenntnis des gemeinsamen Glaubens", *Ökumenische Rundschau* 29/3 (1980), 367-376.

Confessing Our Faith Around the World I, C.S. Song (ed.), Faith and Order Paper No. 104, WCC, Geneva, 1980.

Spirit of God — Spirit of Christ: Ecumenical Reflections on the Filioque Controversy, L. Vischer (ed.), Faith and Order Paper No. 103, WCC, Geneva, 1981.

La théologie du Saint-Esprit dans le dialogue entre l'Orient et l'Occident, sous la direction de L. Vischer, Le Centurion/Les Presses de Taizé, 1981.

Geist Gottes — Geist Christi. Ökumenische Überlegungen zur Filioque-Kontroverse, hg. L. Vischer, Beiheft zur Ökumenischen Rundschau 39, Verlag Otto Lembeck, Frankfurt/Main 1981.

Does Chalcedon Divide or Unite? Towards Convergence in Orthodox Christology, P. Gregorios, W.H. Lazareth & N.A. Nissiotis (eds.), WCC, Geneva, 1981.

Towards Visible Unity: Commission on Faith and Order, Lima 1982. Vol. I: Minutes and Addresses, Section V: *Towards the Common Expression of the Apostolic Faith Today*, M. Kinnamon (ed.), Faith and Order Paper No. 113, WCC, Geneva, 1982, 3-119.

W. Pannenberg, "Die Bedeutung des Bekenntnisses von Nizäa-Konstantinopel für den ökumenischen Dialog heute", *Ökumenische Rundschau* 31 (1982), 129-140.

W. Pannenberg und K. Lehmann, hrsg., *Glaubensbekenntnis und Kirchengemeinschaft: Das Modell des Konzils von Konstantinopel (381)*, Freiburg, 1982.

Schritte zur sichtbaren Einheit. Lima 1982. Sitzung der Kommission für Glauben und Kirchenverfassung, hrsg. H.-G. Link, Beiheft zur *Ökumenischen Rundschau*, Frankfurt/Main, 1983.

Y. Congar, *Diversité et Communion*, Coll. Cogitatio Fidei No. 112, Cerf, Paris, 1982.

Confessing Our Faith Around the World II, H.-G. Link (ed.), Faith and Order Paper No. 120, WCC, Geneva, 1983.

E. Timiadis, *The Nicene Creed: Our Common Faith*, Fortress Press, USA, 1983.

The Roots of Our Common Faith: Faith in the Scriptures and in the Early Church, H.-G. Link (ed.), Faith and Order Paper No. 119, WCC, Geneva, 1984.

Wurzeln unseres gemeinsamen Glaubens. Glaube in der Bibel und in der Alten Kirche, hrsg. H.-G. Link, Frankfurt, 1985.

Confessing Our Faith Around the World III: The Caribbean and Central America, H.-G. Link (ed.), Faith and Order Paper No. 123, WCC, Geneva, 1984.

Y. Congar, *Diversity and Communion*, SCM Press, London, 1984.

Apostolic Faith Today — A Handbook for Study, H.-G. Link (ed.), Faith and Order Paper No. 124, WCC, Geneva, 1985.

Gemeinsam glauben und bekennen — Handbuch zum Apostolischen Glauben, hg. H.-G. Link, Neukirchen-Vluyn/Paderborn, 1987.

Confessing Our Faith Around the World IV: South America, H.-G. Link (ed.), Faith and Order Paper No. 126, WCC, Geneva, 1985.

G. Voss, "Auf dem Weg zu einem gemeinsamen Ausdruck des apostolischen Glaubens heute: ein Studienprojekt", *Una Sancta* 40 (1985), 2-14.

J.M.R. Tillard, *Eglise et Eglises*, Paris, 1985.

Faith and Renewal. Commission on Faith and Order. Stavanger 1985, T.F. Best (ed.), Faith and Order Paper No. 131, WCC, Geneva, 1986, 107-165.

Glaube und Erneuerung. Stavanger 1985, Sitzung der Kommission für Glauben und Kirchenverfassung, hg. G. Gassmann, Beiheft zur *Ökumenischen Rundschau* 55, Frankfurt, 1986, 82-131.

"Foi et constitution. Conférence de Stavanger 1985", *Istina* 31/1 (1986), 50-137.

G. Gassmann, "Towards the Common Confession of the Apostolic Faith", *One in Christ* 21 (1985), 226-237.

Church — Kingdom — World. The Church as Mystery and Prophetic Sign, G. Limouris (ed.), Faith and Order Paper No. 130, WCC, Geneva, 1986.

J.M.R. Tillard, "Koinonia — Sacrament", *One in Christ* 2 (1986), 104-114.

Apostolizität und Ökumene, hrsg. Reinhard Rittner, mit Beiträgen von E.H. Amberg, G. Gassmann, A. Peters und J. Roloff, Hannover, 1987.

G. Limouris, "The Church: A Mystery of Unity in Diversity", *St Vladimir's Theological Quarterly* 31/2 (1987), 123-142.

Confessing One Faith, "Towards an Ecumenical Explication of the Apostolic Faith as Expressed in the Nicene-Constantinopolitan Creed (381)", Faith and Order Paper No. 140, WCC, Geneva, 1987.

Den einen Glauben bekennen, "Auf dem Weg zu einem gemeinsamen Ausdruck des Apostolischen Glaubens auf der Grundlage des Glaubensbekenntnisses von Nizäa-Konstantinopel (381)", Faith and Order Paper No. 140, ÖRK, Genf, 1988.

Confesser la foi commune, "Vers une explication œcuménique de la foi apostolique exprimée dans le Symbole de Nicée-Constantinople (381)", Document de Foi et constitution no. 140, COE, Genève, 1988.

Towards an Ecumenical Explication of the Apostolic Faith as Expressed in the Nicene-Constantinopolitan Creed (381), transl. into Arabic by T. Mitri, ed. Middle East Council of Churches, Beirut, 1989.

A. Gonzáles Montes, *La fe apostólica, Diálogo Ecuménico* 22 (1987), 357-363.

J.M.R. Tillard, "L'universel et le local", *Irénikon* 60 (1987), 483-494.

M.F.G. Parmentier, "Gemeinsames Bekenntnis als Voraussetzung konziliarer Gemeinschaft der Kirchen", *Internationale Kirchliche Zeitschrift* 77 (1987), 209-222.

Confessing One Faith. A Guide for Ecumenical Study, Commission on Faith and Order, National Council of Churches of Christ, Cincinnati, Ohio, USA, 1988.

Creation and the Kingdom of God. Consultation with Faith and Order, D. Gosling and G. Limouris (eds.), Church and Society Documents, No. 5 (August 1988).

J. Gros, "The Pilgrimage Towards Common Confession", *Ecumenical Trends* 17 (1988), 121-123.

T.F. Torrance, *The Trinitarian Faith*, T. & T. Clark Ltd, Edinburgh, 1988.

Apostolic Faith in America, Th. D. Horgan (ed.), Commission on Faith and Order, NCCC/USA, Grand Rapids, 1988.

Black Witness to the Apostolic Faith, D.T. Shannon and G.S. Wilmore (eds.), Commission on Faith and Order, NCCC/USA, Grand Rapids, 1988.

124   *Confessing the One Faith*

One God — One Lord — One Spirit. On the Explication of the Apostolic Faith Today, H.-G. Link (ed.), Faith and Order Paper No. 139, WCC, Geneva, 1988.

"Ein Gott — ein Herr — ein Geist. Zur Auslegung des apostolischen Glaubens heute", hrsg. H.-G. Link, Beiheft zur *Ökumenischen Rundschau* 56, Frankfurt, 1987.

J. Maraschin, *O Espelho e a Transparência, O Credo Niceno-Konstantinopolitano e a teologia latino-americana*, Rio de Janeiro, 1989.

R. Schäfer, "Die Einheit der Kirche im Studiendokument Den einen Glauben bekennen", *Ökumenische Rundschau* 38 (1989), 47-61.

H. Schütte, *Auf dem Weg zu einem gemeinsamen Ausdruck des apostolischen Glauben heute*, Catholica 43 (1989), 209-230.

J.M.R. 1 ard, "Confesser ensemble la foi apostolique", *Documentation Catholique* 86 (1 9), 967-970.

G. Limouris, "The Integrity of Creation in a World of Change Today", *Theologia* 61/1-2 (1990), 3-30.

J.M.R. Tillard, "Spirit, Reconciliation Church", *The Ecumenical Review* 42/3-4 (1990), 237-249.

Papers presented on "Confessing the Apostolic Faith Together" from different perspectives at the Faith and Order Commission, Budapest, Hungary, August 1989 (by J.M.R. Tillard, Ursula Radke, Lorna Khoo), *Faith and Order 1985-1989. The Commission Meeting at Budapest 1989*, T.F. Best (ed.), Faith and Order Paper No. 148, WCC, Geneva, 1990, 104-126.

Glauben und Kirchenverfassung 1985-1989. Die Tagung der Kommission in Budapest, hrsg. G. Gassmann, Beiheft zur *Ökumenischen Rundschau*, Frankfurt, 1990.

Baptism, Eucharist and Ministry 1982-1990. Report on the Process and Responses, Faith and Order Paper No. 149, WCC, Geneva, 1990.

Die Diskussion über Taufe, Eucharistie und Amt 1982-1990, Frankfurt/Paderborn, 1990.

Come, Holy Spirit — Renew the Whole Creation. An Orthodox Approach, G. Limouris (ed.), Holy Cross Press, Brookline/MA, USA, 1990.

Justice, Peace and Integrity of Creation. Orthodox Insights, G. Limouris (ed.), WCC, Geneva, 1990.

Icons — Windows on Eternity. Theology and Spirituality in Colour (on the occasion of the 1200th anniversary of the Seventh Ecumenical Council in 1987), G. Limouris (ed.), Faith and Order Paper No. 147, WCC, Geneva, 1990.

G. Limouris, "Confessing Christ Yesterday and Today: A Christological Exploration", in *Orthodoxes Forum* 1 (1991), 23-30.

Participants in Consultations on the Apostolic Faith Study

Many are those who have contributed in different capacities to this study, but the following have participated from January 1981 to December 1990 in a series of international consultations and meetings organized by the Faith and Order Commission, and in the drafting process of the present document, as members of the Faith and Order Commission, of the Apostolic Faith Steering Group or as consultants.

Faith and Order Standing Commission, Annecy/France, 3-10 January 1981

Working Group on "Towards the Common Expression of the Apostolic Faith Today"

Rev. Prof. J.M.R. Tillard OP (Roman Catholic Church), Canada — Moderator
Prof. Ivar Asheim (Church of Norway), Norway
Protopresbyter Prof. Vitaly Borovoy (Russian Orthodox Church), USSR/Switzerland
Prof. John Deschner (United Methodist Church), USA
Prof. Dr Anton Houtepen (Roman Catholic Church), Netherlands
Prof. Keiji Ogawa (United Church of Christ in Japan), Japan

F&O staff
Rev. Dr William H. Lazareth (Lutheran Church in America)
Rev. Dr Hans-Georg Link (EKD: United)

Consultation on "Towards the Common Expression of the Apostolic Faith Today", Chambésy/Switzerland, 28 June-4 July 1981

Metropolitan Prof. Damaskinos of Tranoupolis (Ecumenical Patriarchate), Switzerland
Prof. John Deschner (United Methodist Church), USA
Principal Sigqibo Dwane (Church of the Province of Southern Africa), South Africa

Dr Adolfo Ham (Presbyterian-Reformed Church), Cuba
Prof. Gerassimos Konidaris† (Church of Greece), Greece (October 1987)
Prof. Ulrich Kühn (Federation of Evangelical Churches in the GDR: Lutheran),
GDR
Prof. Gregor Larentzakis (Greek Orthodox Archdiocese of Austria/ Ecumenical
Patriarchate), Austria
Rev. Dr John Mbiti (Swiss Protestant Church Federation), Switzerland
Prof. Wolfhart Pannenberg (EKD: Lutheran), FRG
Rev. Prof. Samuel Rayan (Roman Catholic Church), India
Rev. Dr William G. Rusch (Lutheran Church in America), USA
Frère Max Thurian (Reformed Church of France), France
Rev. Prof. J.M.R. Tillard OP (Roman Catholic Church), Canada

F&O staff
Rev. Dr William H. Lazareth
Rev. Dr Hans-Georg Link
(Mrs Renate Sbeghen)

**Consultation on "The Ecumenical Importance of the Nicene Creed",
Odessa/USSR, 9-15 October 1981**

Bishop Mesrob Ashjian (Armenian Apostolic Church of America), Lebanon/USA
Prof. Robert W. Bertram (Lutheran Church-Missouri Synod), USA
Dr (Ms) Ellen Flesseman-van Leer (Reformed Church of Netherlands), Nether-
lands
Rev. Fr René Girault (Roman Catholic Church), France
Rev. Prof. Thomas Hopko (Orthodox Church in America), USA
Dr Yoshiro Ishida (Lutheran World Federation), Switzerland
Prof. Gerassimos Konidaris† (Church of Greece), Greece (October 1987)
Prof. Nicolas Lossky (Russian Orthodox Church), France
Rev. Leonid Nedaikhlebov (Russian Orthodox Church), USSR
Rev. Dr Timothy Njoya (Presbyterian Church of East Africa), Kenya
Dr Kjell Ove Nilsson (Church of Sweden), Sweden
Rev. Victor Petlychenko (Russian Orthodox Church), USSR
Prof. Nikolaij Poltoratsky (Russian Orthodox Church), USSR
Prof. V.C. Samuel (Syrian Orthodox Church of the East), India
Dr Martin Seils (Federation of Evangelical Churches in the GDR: Lutheran),
GDR
Prof. Josef Smolik (Evangelical Church of the Czech Brethren), CSSR
Rev. Prof. Livery Voronov (Russian Orthodox Church), USSR
Prof. Günter Wagner (Baptist Church), Switzerland
Prof. Geoffrey Wainwright (Methodist Church of Great Britain), USA

F&O staff
Rev. Dr Hans-Georg Link
(Mrs Renate Sbeghen)

Faith and Order Plenary Commission, Lima/Peru, 2-15 January 1982

Plenary Commission and working groups discuss and adopt plans for the Apostolic Faith Study

Consultation on "The Apostolic Faith in the Scriptures and in the Early Church", Rome/Italy, 1-8 October 1983

Rev. Prof. Raymond E. Brown (Roman Catholic Church), USA
Rev. Janet Crawford (Church of the Province of New Zealand), New Zealand
Prof. John Deschner (United Methodist Church), USA — Moderator
Prof. Kwesi Dickson (Methodist Church), Ghana
Dr (Ms) Ellen Flesseman-van Leer (Netherlands Reformed Church), Netherlands
Rev. Dr Günther Gassmann (EKD: Lutheran), Switzerland
Prof. E. Glenn Hinson (Southern Baptist Convention), USA
Mgr Prof. Aloys Klein (Roman Catholic Church), Vatican
Prof. Georg Kretschmar (EKD: Lutheran), FRG
Dom Emmanuel Lanne (Roman Catholic Church), Belgium
Dr Jorge Pantelis (Methodist Church), Bolivia
Rev. Dr Horace O. Russell (Jamaica Baptist Union), Jamaica
Prof. V.C. Samuel (Syrian Orthodox Church of the East), India
Prof. Günter Wagner (Baptist Church), Switzerland
Prof. Geoffrey Wainwright (Methodist Church of Great Britain), USA
Prof. Michael Wyschogrod (Jewish Community), USA
Prof. John D. Zizioulas (Ecumenical Patriarchate), Scotland

F&O staff
V. Rev. Dr Gennadios Limouris (Ecumenical Patriarchate)
Rev. Dr Hans-Georg Link
Prof. Todor Sabev (Bulgarian Orthodox Church)
Frère Max Thurian
(Mrs Renate Sbeghen)

Faith and Order Standing Commission, Crete/Greece, 6-14 April 1984

Appointment of Steering Group on Apostolic Faith Study

Rev. Prof. J.M.R. Tillard OP (Roman Catholic Church), Canada — Moderator
Metropolitan Dr Bartholomew of Philadelphia (Ecumenical Patriarchate), Turkey
Prof. John Deschner (United Methodist Church), USA
Prof. Ulrich Kühn (Federation of Evangelical Churches in the GDR: Lutheran), GDR

Rev. Dr Jaci Maraschin (Episcopal Church), Brazil
Prof. Wolfhart Pannenberg (EKD: Lutheran), FRG
Rev. Dr Horace O. Russell (Jamaica Baptist Union), Jamaica
Mrs Mary Tanner (Church of England), England
Dean Yemba Kekumba (Church of Christ in Zaire — Methodist Community),
    Zaire

F&O staff
Rev. Dr Günther Gassmann (EKD: Lutheran)
Rev. Dr Hans-Georg Link
V. Rev. Dr Gennadios Limouris
(Mrs Renate Sbeghen)

Consultation on the second article of the Creed, "We believe in one Lord Jesus Christ", Kottayam/India, 14-22 November 1984

Dr (Ms) Roberta Bondi (United Methodist Church), USA
Rev. Janet Crawford (Church of the Province of New Zealand), New Zealand
V. Rev. Prof. George Dragas (Greek Orthodox Archdiocese of Thyateira and
    Great Britain/Ecumenical Patriarchate), England
Rev. Dr K.M. George (Syrian Orthodox Church of the East), India
Metropolitan Dr Paulos Mar Gregorios (Syrian Orthodox Church of the East),
    India
Rev. Dr B.H. Jackaya (United Evangelical-Lutheran Churches in India), India
Rev. Dr O.V. Jathanna (Church of South India), India
Rev. Dr M.J. Joseph (Mar Thoma Syrian Church of Malabar), India
Ms Marianne Katoppo (Reformed Church), Indonesia
Rev. Fr Joseph Koikakudy (Roman Catholic Church), India
Rev. Fr Jacob Kollaparambil (Roman Catholic Church), India
Prof. Ulrich Kühn (Federation of Evangelical Churches in the GDR: Lutheran),
    GDR/Austria
Dr Moises Mendez (Baptist Union), Mexico
Metropolitan Mar Ostathios (Syrian Orthodox Church of the East), India
Rev. Dr Rienzi Perera (Anglican Church), Sri Lanka
Prof. Dietrich Ritschl (EKD: Reformed), FRG
Ms Vimla Subaiya (Church of North India), India
Prof. Rowan Williams (Church of England), England

F&O staff
Rev. Dr Günther Gassmann
Rev. Dr Hans-Georg Link
(Mrs Renate Sbeghen)

Consultation on the third article of the Creed, "We believe in the Holy Spirit, the Church and the Life of the World to Come", Chantilly/ France, 3-10 January 1985

Prof. Torleiv Austad (Church of Norway), Norway
President Edward Czaijko (United Evangelical Church), Poland
Prof. John Deschner (United Methodist Church), USA
Prof. Hermann Goltz (Federation of Evangelical Churches in the GDR: Lutheran), GDR
Rev. Prof. Thomas Hopko (Orthodox Church in America), USA
Prof. (Ms) Sung-Hee Lee (Presbyterian Church in Korea), Korea
Dr (Ms) Ann L. Loades (Church of England), England
Prof. Per Lønning (Church of Norway), Norway/France
Prof. Werner Löser (Roman Catholic Church), FRG
Prof. Nicolas Lossky (Russian Orthodox Church), France
Prof. (Ms) Lauree Hersch Meyer (Church of the Brethren), USA
Prof. Jürgen Moltmann (EKD: Reformed), FRG
Rev. Dr Martin Parmentier (Old Catholic Church), Netherlands
Prof. Janos Pasztor (Reformed Church in Hungary), Hungary
Rev. Fr Michael Putney (Roman Catholic Church), New Zealand/Italy
Dr Michael Root (Lutheran Church in America), USA
Rev. Dr Horace O. Russell (Jamaica Baptist Union), Jamaica
Mrs Veronica Swai (Evangelical-Lutheran Church in Tanzania), Tanzania
Rev. Prof. J.M.R. Tillard OP (Roman Catholic Church), Canada — Moderator
Prof. Wolfgang Ullmann (Federation of Evangelical Churches in the GDR: Lutheran), GDR
Rev. Prof. Livery Voronov (Russian Orthodox Church), USSR

F&O staff
Rev. Dr Günther Gassmann
Rev. Dr Hans-Georg Link
Frère Max Thurian
Vikar Dietrich Werner (Intern) (EKD: Lutheran)
(Mrs Renate Sbeghen)

Consultation on the first article of the Creed, "We believe in one God", Kinshasa/Zaire, 14-22 March 1985

Rev. Fr John K.A. Aniagwu (Roman Catholic Church), Nigeria
Prof. Dan-Ilie Ciobotea (Romanian Orthodox Church), Switzerland
Prof. Sigurd Daecke (EKD: Lutheran), FRG
Rev. Dr Efefe Elonda (Church of Christ in Zaire — Disciples of Christ), Zaire
Prof. Alasdair Heron (Church of Scotland), Scotland/FRG

Rev. Jonah Lwanga (Greek Archdiocese of Irinoupolis/Greek Orthodox Patri-
archate of Alexandria), Kenya
Mgr Monsengwo Pasinya (Roman Catholic Church), Zaire
Dr Kjell Ove Nilsson (Church of Sweden), Sweden
Prof. Peder Nørgaard-Højen (Church of Denmark), Denmark
Mrs Rosemary Nthamburi (Methodist Church), Kenya
Prof. Owanga-Welo (Kimbanguist Church), Zaire
Mrs Mary Tanner (Church of England), England
Prof. Günter Wagner (Baptist Church), Switzerland
Prof. Geoffrey Wainwright (Methodist Church of Great Britain), USA
Dean Yemba Kekumba (Church of Christ in Zaire — Methodist Community),
Zaire

F&O staff
Rev. Dr Günther Gassmann
Rev. Dr Hans-Georg Link
(Mrs Renate Sbeghen)

**Meeting of the Apostolic Faith Steering Group, Crêt-Bérard/Switzerland,
28 May-2 June 1985**

Rev. Prof. J.M.R. Tillard OP — Moderator
Prof. John Deschner
Prof. Ulrich Kühn
Rev. Dr Jaci Maraschin
Prof. Wolfhart Pannenberg
Rev. Dr Horace O. Russell
Mrs Mary Tanner
Dean Yemba Kekumba

F&O staff
Rev. Dr Günther Gassmann
V. Rev. Dr. Gennadios Limouris
Rev. Dr Hans-Georg Link
Frère Max Thurian
(Mrs Renate Sbeghen)

**Faith and Order Plenary Commission, Stavanger/Norway,
13-25 August 1985**

Plenary Commission and five working groups discuss and revise the draft on
"Explication" on Apostolic Faith

Faith and Order/Church and Society Consultation, York/England, 1-4 May 1986

Dr (Ms) Svein Aage Christoffersen (Church of Norway), Norway
Mr Martin Conway (Church of England), England
V. Rev. Prof. George Dragas (Greek Orthodox Archdiocese of Thyateira and Great Britain/Ecumenical Patriarchate), England
Rev. Prof. Duncan Forrester (Church of Scotland), Scotland
Most Rev. John Habgood (Church of England), England
Prof. Dr Anton Houtepen (Roman Catholic Church), Netherlands
Prof. Jürgen Hübner (Evangelical Church in Germany: United), FRG
Rev. Fr Michael Hurley (Roman Catholic Church), Ireland
Rev. Dr Laurentius Klein (Roman Catholic Church), FRG
Dr (Ms) Mady Laeyendecker-Thung, Netherlands
Prof. Einar Sigurbjörnsson (Church of Iceland), Iceland

WCC staff
Rev. Dr Günther Gassmann
Rev. Dr David Gosling (Sub-unit on Church and Society)
Rev. Dr Hans-Georg Link

Meeting of the Apostolic Faith Steering Group, West Berlin/FRG, 9-12 July 1986

Rev. Prof. J.M.R. Tillard OP — Moderator
Prof. John Deschner
Prof. Ulrich Kühn
Rev. Dr Jaci Maraschin
Prof. Wolfhart Pannenberg
Rev. Dr Horace O. Russell
Mrs Mary Tanner
Prof. Evangelos Theodorou (Church of Greece) (new member)
Dean Yemba Kekumba

F&O staff
Rev. Dr Günther Gassmann
V. Rev. Dr Gennadios Limouris
Rev. Dr Hans-Georg Link
Frère Max Thurian
(Mrs Renate Sbeghen)

Meeting of the Apostolic Faith Steering Group, Paris/France, 21-27 April 1987

Rev. Prof. J.M.R. Tillard OP — Moderator
Prof. John Deschner

Rev. Dr Jaci Maraschin
Prof. Peder Nørgaard-Højen (Church of Denmark), Consultant
Prof. Wolfhart Pannenberg
Mrs Mary Tanner
Prof. Evangelos Theodorou
Dr Morris West (Baptist Union of Great Britain and Ireland), Consultant
Dean Yemba Kekumba

F&O staff
Rev. Dr Günther Gassmann
Rev. Dr Irmgard Kindt (EKD: Lutheran)
V. Rev. Dr Gennadios Limouris
Mr Hinrich Witzel (intern) (EKD: Lutheran)
(Mrs Renate Sbeghen)

Consultation on "The Doctrine of Creation and Its Integrity — A Challenge to the Responsibility of Christianity Today", Porto Alegre/Brazil, 13-20 November 1987

Rev. Joao Guilhermo Biehl (Evangelical Church of Lutheran Confession in Brazil), Brazil
Rev. Dr Alain Blancy (Reformed Church of France), France
V. Rev. Prof. Alkiviadis Calivas (Greek Orthodox Archdiocese of North and South America/Ecumenical Patriarchate), USA
Rev. Cornelia Coenen-Marx (Evangelical Church in Germany: United), FRG
Rev. Dr German Correa (Roman Catholic Church), Colombia
Dr (Ms) Beatriz Melano Couch (Presbyterian Church), Argentina
Prof. John Deschner (United Methodist Church), USA — Moderator
V. Rev. Prof. George Dragas (Greek Orthodox Archdiocese of Thyateira and Great Britain/Ecumenical Patriarchate), England
Rev. Dr Ion Dura (Romanian Orthodox Church), Belgium
Ms Ana L. de Garcia (Lutheran Church), Costa Rica
Rev. (Ms) Gladis Gassen (Evangelical Church of Lutheran Confession in Brazil), Brazil
Brother Jeffrey Gros (Roman Catholic Church), USA
Ms Gisela von Heusinger (Evangelical Church in Germany: United), FRG/ Switzerland
Ms Rose Jarjour (National Evangelical Synod of Syria and Lebanon), Cyprus
Rev. Roberto Jordan (Reformed Church), Argentina
Rev. Prof. David Kapkin (Roman Catholic Church), Colombia
Rev. Fr Leonardo Martin (Roman Catholic Church), Brazil
V. Rev. Orlando Santos Oliveira (Episcopal Church), Brazil
Prof. Milan Opocensky (Evangelical Church of the Czech Brethren), Czechoslovakia

Rev. Dr Horace O. Russell (Jamaica Baptist Union), Jamaica
Rev. Dr David Trickett (United Methodist Church), USA
Rev. Dr Vitor Westhelle (Evangelical Church of Lutheran Confession in Brazil), Brazil
Rev. Dr (Ms) Patricia Wilson-Kastner (Episcopal Church), USA
Dean Yemba Kekumba (Church of Christ in Zaire — Methodist Community), Zaire

WCC staff
Rev. Georgij Glouchik (Russian Orthodox Church), "Justice, Peace and the Integrity of Creation" Office
Rev. Dr David Gosling (Church of England), Sub-unit on "Church and Society"

F&O staff
Rev. Dr Günther Gassmann
V. Rev. Dr Gennadios Limouris
(Mrs Renate Sbeghen)

Interpreters: Mrs Elisabeth Delmonte
Mrs Susana K. de Haynal

Consultation on "Confessing the Crucified and Risen Christ in the Social, Cultural and Ethical Context of Today", Rhodes/Greece, 4-10 January 1988

Dr Charles Amjad-Ali (Church of Pakistan), Pakistan
Metropolitan Dr Bartholomew of Philadelphia (Ecumenical Patriarchate), Turkey
Rev. Fr Frans Bouwen (Roman Catholic Church), Israel
Rt Rev. Manas Buthelezi (Evangelical Lutheran Church in Southern Africa), South Africa
Archpriest Prof. Nikolai Chivarov (Bulgarian Orthodox Church), Bulgaria
V. Rev. Prof. Dimitrios J. Constantelos (Greek Orthodox Archdiocese of North and South America/Ecumenical Patriarchate), USA
Rev. Fr Jean Corbon (Roman Catholic Church), Lebanon
Prof. John Deschner (United Methodist Church), USA
Rev. Dr (Ms) Julia Gatta (Episcopal Church), USA
Rev. Dr (Ms) Beverley Gaventa (Disciples of Christ), USA
Brother Jeffrey Gros (Roman Catholic Church), USA
Prof. Mark S. Heim (American Baptist Churches), USA
Rev. Prof. Walter Kasper (Roman Catholic Church), FRG
Rev. (Ms) Lorna Khoo (Methodist Church), Singapore
Dr (Ms) Dimitra Koukoura (Church of Greece), Greece
Prof. Ulrich Kühn (Federation of Evangelical Churches in the GDR: Lutheran), GDR
Prof. (Ms) Hung-See Lee (Presbyterian Church of Korea), FRG

Prof. Nicolas Lossky (Russian Orthodox Church), France
Dr (Ms) Eeva Martikainen (Evangelical Lutheran Church of Finland), Finland
Rev. Odair Pedroso Mateus (Presbyterian Church), Brazil
Prof. Alexei Ossipov (Russian Orthodox Church), USSR
Prof. Wolfhart Pannenberg (Evangelical Church in Germany: Lutheran), FRG
Rev. Dr Martin F.G. Parmentier (Old Catholic Church), Netherlands
Prof. Dietrich Ritschl (Evangelical Church in Germany: Reformed), FRG
V. Rev. Prof. John Romanides (Church of Greece), Greece
Rev. Dr William G. Rusch (Evangelical Lutheran Church in America), USA
Rev. Dr Horace O. Russell (Jamaica Baptist Union), Jamaica
Prof. Josef Smolik (Evangelical Church of the Czech Brethren), Czechoslovakia
Mrs Mary Tanner (Church of England), England
Rev. Prof. J.M.R. Tillard OP (Roman Catholic Church), Canada — Moderator
Dr Andreas Tillyrides (Church of Cyprus), Kenya
Dean Yemba Kekumba (Church of Christ in Zaire — Methodist Community),
    Zaire

WCC staff
Prof. John Pobee (Church of the Province of West Africa, Anglican), Sub-unit on
    Programme for Theological Education

F&O staff
Rev. Dr Günther Gassmann
Rev. Dr Irmgard Kindt
V. Rev. Dr Gennadios Limouris
(Mrs Renate Sbeghen)

Interpreter: Ms Nathalia Chernyk

Faith and Order/Church and Society Consultation on "Creation and the Kingdom of God", Dublin/Ireland, 6-10 May 1988

Ms Julia Brosnan (Roman Catholic Church), England
Rev. Fr Denis Carroll (Roman Catholic Church), Ireland
Mr Richard G. Chambers (United Church of Canada), Canada
Rev. J.T.K. Daniel (Church of South India), India
V. Rev. Prof. Dr George Dragas (Greek Orthodox Archdiocese of Thyateira and
    Great Britain/Ecumenical Patriarchate), England
Rev. Alan D. Falconer (Church of Scotland), Scotland/Ireland
Rev. Prof. Duncan Forrester (Church of Scotland), Scotland
Rev. Dr Gordon Gray (Presbyterian Church in Ireland), Ireland
V. Rev. Canon Prof. D.W. Hardy (Church of England), England
Fr Michael Hurley (Roman Catholic Church), Ireland
Rev. David Kerr (Methodist Church in Ireland), N. Ireland
Archbishop Dr Aram Keshishian (Armenian Apostolic Church, Cilicia), Lebanon
    — Moderator

Dr (Ms) Dimitra Koukoura (Church of Greece), Greece
Ms Marilia Leao (Methodist Church in Brazil), Brazil
Dr John May (Roman Catholic Church), Ireland
Rev. (Ms) Martine Millet (Reformed Church of France), France
Sister Nektaria Paradissi (Church of Greece), Greece/Ireland
Rev. Dr Kjell Ove Nilsson (Church of Sweden), Sweden
Dr (Ms) Turid Karlsen Seim (Church of Norway), Norway
Rev. Arnold Temple (Methodist Church), Ireland
Rev. Dr (Ms) Patricia Wilson-Kastner (Episcopal Church), USA

WCC staff
Rev. Dr David Gosling (Sub-unit on Church and Society)
V. Rev. Prof. Dr Gennadios Limouris (Faith and Order)
Rev. Dr Freda Rajotte (Sub-unit on Church and Society)
(Ms Barbara Loheyde)

**Consultation on "Ecclesiology — Basic Ecumenical Perspectives",
Pyatigorsk/USSR, 22-29 November 1988**

Rev. Canon Leopold Ankrah (Anglican Church), Liberia
Mr Sergei Bestchastniy (Russian Orthodox Church), USSR
Dr (Ms) Roberta Bondi (United Methodist Church), USA
Rev. Prof. Emmanuel Clapsis (Greek Orthodox Archdiocese of North and South
    America/Ecumenical Patriarchate), USA
Rev. Martin Cressey (United Reformed Church), England
Prof. John Deschner (United Methodist Church), USA
Rt Rev. Prof. Noah K. Dzobo (Presbyterian Church in Ghana), Ghana
Archpriest Georgij Glouchik (Russian Orthodox Church), USSR
Archpriest Prof. Nikolai Gundiaev (Russian Orthodox Church), USSR
Prof. E. Glenn Hinson (Southern Baptist Convention), USA
Rev. Prof. Thomas Hopko (Orthodox Church in America), USA
Rev. Roberto Jordan (Presbyterian Church), Argentina
Rev. Dr Abraham Kuruvilla (Mar Thoma Syrian Church), India
Prof. Nicolas Lossky (Russian Orthodox Church), France
Dr (Ms) Zenaida P. Lumba (Methodist Church), Philippines
Rev. Jalongos M. Manullang (Batak Protestant Christian Church (Lutheran)),
    Indonesia
Prof. (Ms) Lauree Hersch Meyer (Church of the Brethren), USA
Sister Mary O'Driscoll (Roman Catholic Church), Vatican
Prof. Alexei Ossipov (Russian Orthodox Church), USSR
Ms Olga Ponamareva (Russian Orthodox Church), USSR
Mgr John Radano (Roman Catholic Church), Vatican
Prof. John Reumann (Evangelical Lutheran Church in America), USA
Prof. Paolo Ricca (Waldensian Church), Italy

V. Rev. Prof. John Romanides (Church of Greece), Greece
Bishop Dr Paul-Werner Scheele (Roman Catholic Church), FRG
Archpriest Vassili Stoikov (Russian Orthodox Church), USSR
Rev. Livingstone Thompson (Moravian Church in Jamaica), Jamaica
Rev. Prof. J.M.R. Tillard OP (Roman Catholic Church), Canada
Prof. Wolfgang Ullmann (Federation of Evangelical Churches in the GDR: Lutheran), GDR
Prof. (Ms) Dorothea Wendebourg (Evangelical Church in Germany: Lutheran), FRG

F&O staff
Rev. Dr Thomas F. Best
Rev. Dr Günther Gassmann
V. Rev. Dr Gennadios Limouris
(Mrs Renate Sbeghen)

Interpreters: Ms Natalia Chernyk
Mr Sergei Gordeev
Mr Leonid Nechaev
Ms Zinaida Nosova
Ms Olga Piskunova

Meeting of the Apostolic Faith Steering Group, Rome/Italy, 31 March-4 April 1989

Rev. Prof. J.M.R. Tillard OP — Moderator
Metropolitan Dr Bartholomew of Philadelphia
Prof. John Deschner
Prof. Ulrich Kühn
Prof. (Ms) Sung-Hee Lee-Linke (Presbyterian Church of Korea), new member
Rev. Dr Jaci Maraschin
Prof. Wolfhart Pannenberg
Rev. Dr Horace O. Russell
Dr (Ms) Mary Tanner
Prof. Evangelos Theodorou
Dean Yemba Kekumba

F&O staff
Rev. Dr Günther Gassmann
V. Rev. Dr Gennadios Limouris
(Mrs Renate Sbeghen)

Consultation on "Ecumenical Reflections on the Holy Spirit in Creation, Church and History", Würzburg/FRG, 12-19 June 1989

Dr (Ms) Anna Marie Aagaard (Church of Denmark), Denmark
Rev. (Ms) Eva Brebovszky (Lutheran Church in Hungary), Hungary

Rev. Dr Keith Clements (Baptist Union of Great Britain and Ireland), England
Rev. Dr Lothar Coenen (Evangelical Church in Germany: Reformed), FRG
Dr Erskil Frank (Church of Sweden), Sweden
Dr (Ms) Käte Gaede (Federation of Evangelical Churches in the GDR), GDR
Rev. (Ms) Jacqueline Grant (African Methodist Episcopal Church), USA
Rev. Canon Prof. D.W. Hardy (Church of England), England
Rev. Istvan Karasszon (Reformed Church in Hungary), Hungary
Rev. Prof. Edward Kilmartin SJ (Roman Catholic Church), Vatican
Mgr Prof. Aloys Klein (Roman Catholic Church), FRG
Prof. Gregor Larentzakis (Archdiocese of Austria/Ecumenical Patriarchate),
   Austria
Dr (Ms) Käthe La Roche (Swiss Protestant Church Federation), Switzerland
Prof. (Ms) Sung-Hee Lee-Linke (Presbyterian Church of Korea), FRG
Rev. Dr Harald Malschitzky (Evangelical Church of Lutheran Confession in
   Brazil), Brazil
Rev. (Ms) Martine Millet (Reformed Church in France), France
Prof. Munduku Ngamayamu (Church of Christ in Zaire), Zaire
Rev. Samuel A. Piringer (Evangelical Church of the Augsburg Confession in the
   Socialist Republic of Romania), Romania
Rev. L.H. Purwanto (Gereja Kristen Indonesia (Reformed)), Indonesia/Nether-
   lands
Rev. Dr Robert F. Smith (United Church in Canada), Canada
Bishop Dr Paul-Werner Scheele (Roman Catholic Church), FRG
Prof. Hans-Joachim Schulz (Roman Catholic Church), FRG
Rev. Prof. J.M.R. Tillard OP (Roman Catholic Church), Canada — Moderator
Rev. (Ms) Marja J. van der Veen-Schenkeveld (Reformed Churches in the
   Netherlands), Netherlands

F&O staff
Rev. Dr Günther Gassmann
V. Rev. Dr Gennadios Limouris
(Ms Margot Wahl, Administrative Assistant)

Interpreters: Ms Renate Sbeghen
Ms Helga Voigt

Faith and Order Plenary Commission, Budapest/Hungary, 9-21 August 1989

Plenary Commission and working groups discuss the study document "Confessing
One Faith" and make comments and suggestions for further revision to be passed
on to Apostolic Faith Steering Group.

Meeting of the Apostolic Faith Steering Group, Oxford/England, 3-10 January 1990

Rev. Prof. J.M.R. Tillard OP — Moderator
Rev. Dr Keith Clements — Consultant
Prof. John Deschner
Prof. Ulrich Kühn
Prof. (Ms) Sung-Hee Lee-Linke
Rev. Dr Jaci Maraschin
Prof. Wolfhart Pannenberg
Dr (Ms) Mary Tanner
Prof. Evangelos Theodorou
Dean Yemba Kekumba

F&O staff
Ms Ursula Gieseke (intern)
V. Rev. Dr Gennadios Limouris
(Mrs Renate Sbeghen)

Meeting of the Apostolic Faith Steering Group, Venice/Italy, 3-11 April 1990

Rev. Prof. J.M.R. Tillard OP — Moderator
Rev. Dr Keith Clements — Consultant
Prof. Ulrich Kühn
Prof. (Ms) Hung-See Lee-Linke
Rev. Dr Jaci Maraschin
Prof. Wolfhart Pannenberg
Rev. Dr Horace O. Russell
Dr (Ms) Mary Tanner
Rev. Prof. Paul Tarazi (Greek Orthodox Patriarchate of Antioch), Consultant
Prof. Geoffrey Wainwright (Methodist Church of Great Britain), Consultant
Dean Yemba Kekumba

F&O staff
Rev. Dr Günther Gassmann
V. Rev. Dr Gennadios Limouris
(Mrs Renate Sbeghen)

Meeting of the Apostolic Faith Steering Group, Dunblane/Scotland, 14-16 August 1990

Rev. Prof. J.M.R. Tillard OP — Moderator
Metropolitan Dr Bartholomew of Chalcedon
Prof. John Deschner

Prof. Wolfhart Pannenberg
Rev. Dr Horace O. Russell
Dr (Ms) Mary Tanner
Prof. Evangelos Theodorou
Dean Yemba Kekumba

F&O staff
V. Rev. Dr Gennadios Limouris
(Mrs Renate Sbeghen)

Faith and Order Standing Commission, Dunblane/Scotland, 16-24 August 1990

The Standing Commission approved the study document on "Confessing the One Faith" and authorized its publication in order to be sent officially to the churches for further study and consideration and to be made available to the wider ecumenical movement.

Editorial Meeting, Rome/Italy, 15-17 December 1990

Prof. Wolfhart Pannenberg
Dr (Ms) Mary Tanner
Rev. Prof. J.M.R. Tillard — Moderator

F&O staff
Rev. Dr Günther Gassmann
V. Rev. Dr Gennadios Limouris